HEAT

Series 3 Number 1

Ben Juers
Untitled, 2021
One colour linocut
Black block ink on 120gsm
printmaking paper

Editorial

IT IS AN HONOUR to be relaunching HEAT after a decade-long hiatus, with five such distinguished writers. At the close of our second series, print seemed to be firmly on the way out. 'The electronic medium beckons,' the editorial of that last issue declared, 'with its heavenly promise of weightlessness and omnipresence.' And yet here we are: Australia's international literary journal, available once again as a beautiful printed object, albeit a different looking one. We've moved away from the compendium-like issues of the past to a smaller, more intimate conception of the magazine, published every two months, that we hope will travel lightly and defy distraction. Jenny Grigg's design emphasises our new tempo, boldly centring our contributors on the cover, using a tactile minimalism to great effect.

As readers of the first two series will recall, HEAT doesn't follow strict themes; rather, the pieces in each issue form a kind of constellation, despite their differences in voice and perspective. The five writers that appear here draw on worlds as far apart as the Adelaide Hills in South Australia, Mato Grosso do Sul in Brazil, and Lenzing in Austria, with each linked to the others, whether story, essay or poem, by association. One reader will see multifaceted reflections on a disaster and its aftermath; another uncovers words or images that seem singular but later reappear, disconnected but resonant. In 'Death Takes Me', the story that closes these pages, Cristina Rivera Garza imagines the notion of poetry as *a field of action*. To my mind, HEAT too is a field of action, one in which literary integrity is paramount.

Alexandra Christie

MIREILLE JUCHAU

ONLY ONE REFUSED

Mireille Juchau is a novelist, essayist and Walkley Award-winning critic. Her most recent novel *The World Without Us* won the Victorian Premier's Prize. 'Only one refused' was shortlisted in the 2020 Calibre Essay Prize and is part of an ongoing project on the afterlife of war.

Overleaf
Renata Grau, Häftlings-Personal-Karte Mauthausen, DE ITS 1.1.26.8, 56960, ITS Digital Archive, Arolsen Archives.

EVEN AS I UNCOVER materials that suggest Renate's appearance – a portrait of her sister on an East Berlin balcony in 1961, prisoner records from age sixteen till liberation, a Hollerith card that catalogues her physical features – she remains stubbornly abstract, a dream that can't be retrieved. I scan the women photographed at the Mauthausen subcamp and the summer women displaced in southern Italy though I can't possibly recognise the one I'm looking for – Renate Grau. She's an assemblage of Nazi documents, a set of symptoms in a reparations claim, one name on the postwar lists of survivors and displaced persons. Who can make a person from such traces? Despite this scarcity, despite five years of searching, I'm driven to discover more. Sometimes I'm unsure if I'm summoning Renate – an obscuring aura that heralds a migraine, an unquantifiable sensory fact. Sometimes our positions reverse and I feel my self dissipate as her form materialises out of the past. Then I'm haunted, in the ways Avery Gordon describes it, as unresolved social violence erupts directly or obliquely, and '...home becomes unfamiliar...your bearings on the world lose direction...the over-and-done-with comes alive...what's been in your blind field comes into view.'

On Renate's Hollerith card her nose, mouth and ears are classified 'normal'. Her face is oval, her teeth *gut*, her hair is *Schwarz*, her eyes are grey, or Grau like her surname. The card describes a body broken into parts considered suitable for slave labour, a human cog in an industrial system overseen by Deutsche Hollerith-Maschinen, IBM's German subsidiary. Hollerith cards were used by the Nazis to manage their prisoners, and since IBM designed, made and supplied these cards, my portrait of Renate comes courtesy of a Nazi system developed by an American company, via the Mauthausen subcamp in Lenzing, Austria

KL.: Mauthausen

Häftlings-P

Fam.-Name: G r a u

Vorname: Renata

Geb. am: 16.4.27 in: Berlin

Stand: led. Kinder:

Wohnort: Berlin-Scharlottenburg

Strasse: Gustloffstr. 17

Religion: mos. Staatsang.: DR

Wohnort d. Angehörigen: Vater Hubert G. unb.

Eingewiesen am: 17.10.44 Au

durch:

in KL.: KLM

Grund: DR Jüdin

Vorstrafen:

– 3.

am:

am:

am:

am:

am:

am:

am:

mit Ve

Strafen im Lager:

Grund:	Art:

KL. 5/6. 44-500000

ing

onal-Karte

Häftl.-Nr.:	579 DR Jüdin

erstellt
1944
an KL.
hausen

an KL.

an KL.

an KL.

an KL.

an KL.

assung:
durch KL.:

g v.:

Bemerkung:

Personen-Beschreibung:

Grösse: 163 cm
Gestalt: schlank
Gesicht: oval
Augen: grau
Nase: norm.
Mund: norm.
Ohren: norm.
Zähne: gut
Haare: schw.
Sprache: dtsch.

Bes. Kennzeichen:

Charakt.-Eigenschaften:

Sicherheit b. Einsatz:

Körperliche Verfassung:

where Renate did forced labour in 1944. Ten years earlier, a facility using IBM technologies to process the census opened in Berlin. In his speech the manager, Willy Heidinger, prefigured the overblown claims, pseudoscience and lethal administrivia that would characterise the Nazi regime:

> We are very much like the physician, in that we dissect, cell by cell, the German cultural body. We report every individual characteristic…on a little card. These are not dead cards, quite the contrary, they prove later on that they come to life when the cards are sorted at a rate of 25,000 per hour according to the characteristics. These characteristics are grouped like the organs of our cultural body, and they will be calculated and determined with the help of our tabulating machines.

Not dead cards, quite the contrary. The *little card* tells me Renate was 163 centimetres tall – the same height and age my daughter is now. She's slim. With her parents, Hubert and Herta, she joined the 1,388 prisoners transported to Auschwitz on 12 October, 1944. They'd survived sixteen months in Theresienstadt, where 34,000 people had died of malnutrition. At some point Renate contracted tuberculosis. In Auschwitz, her parents were murdered. Soon after this event, which she will later describe as the source of all her suffering, Renate was sent from Auschwitz with 600 Jewish women to Salzkammergut, the mountainous region of Austria. It was just before the brutal winter of 1944. Most women were assigned to the local textile factory, Zellwolle Lenzing AG, to make rayon. From the scant list of dates and places sent to me by the International Tracing Service, I assume Renate, classed as an unskilled worker, was among them. At Lenzing the women worked under Frau

Schmidt, Oberaufseherin Margarete Freinberger and Maria Kunik – each guard trained to recognise work slowdowns, sabotage and to perform something called 'malicious pleasure'. One survivor who witnessed this training recalled that when fifty trainees were instructed to hit a prisoner, 'only three asked the reason why they had to hit the inmate; only three asked the reason why, and only one refused.'

During my childhood I'd sometimes help my mother choose fabric from hundreds of patterned bolts. Her tight domestic budget meant she made most of our clothes, and like the daughters of countless refugees, she'd learned from her parents to sew. While she headed for the subdued cottons, I'd drift away to the novelty buttons and applique lace, to the synthetics, where my uncertain face would appear, distorted in the sheen. Choosing material was one of the few things I did alone with my mother, whose father once sold fabric in a Berlin department store until it was Aryanised, though I didn't know this then. My mother rarely spoke about her childhood, or her parents' lives. Later, I associated this silence with the years of hiding her background in a culture that preferred neither Germans or Jews, and called this erasure assimilation, so I can't help thinking that the muted fabrics she preferred were an extension of this passing. I would not be the kid in flammable nylon at parties or barbecues, better to fade out, or blend in. When asked if I think of myself as Jewish, a strange uncertainty overcomes me and I wonder about the false self that assimilation demands, a self which still must pass as real. I wonder what this performance might have cost my mother. Over time I've grown nostalgic for those fabric shops with their bread-and-camphor scent, just as my mother, while choosing fabric, perhaps reprised the suburban dress shop her parents ran decades before. Now, after researching Lenzing Zellwolle, when I pass my local Fabric City with its bright rayons stacked on the street I detect only a toxic base note.

At some point in this childhood I heard about Renate, my grandmother's cousin, who was living back then in Tel Aviv under another name. I was told she was 'damaged', and since liberation, preferred not to be visited by any surviving family. Maybe because I'd developed a liking for solitude, and a habit of drifting into epic silences, I was privately awed at Renate's demand, and what I understood to be her radical isolation. I didn't know how to voice any wish, least of all a wish to be left alone by my family. The word *damage* stood out most particularly when my grandmother used Renate's diminutive name, Reni. In a name-based synaesthesia, I pictured someone slight, fondly regarded, incompatible with harm. Later, I convinced myself her isolation must have been a form of courage and independence. I interpreted every fact through a teenage solipsism, yet I sensed something askew in this history. I hadn't registered the way family stories rigidly fix us in the group and in the world they claim to describe – like a mirror in which we expect to see ourselves but find only an empty double veering from our surroundings.

Of all my grandparents' stories about life before and after exile, it was Reni's that took hold of me. So I requested everything the International Tracing Service had about the Graus. Eventually I received the Nazi records of Renate's twelve years of persecution including the Hollerith card, and the lists titled *Sh'erit ha-Pletah* (surviving remnant) of the Jews who survived. Since my grandmother's death there's no one left in my family who can describe the precise nature of Renate's injuries, though I'd always sensed these were more psychological than physical. Renate was absorbed into my childhood *why*, that answerless word, engine of my days. The mystery of Renate became inseparable from the mysteries of existence and, it seems to me now, from the puzzle of my self.

As I read about the carbon disulphide used in the factory at Lenzing, I began to wonder if this work was the partial cause of Renate's 'damage' – the dangers of working with the chemical were already known in the nineteenth century when neurologist Jean-Martin Charcot linked it to hysteria. In *Fake Silk*, Paul David Blanc includes Charcot's account of a man working in rubber production collapsing with 'toxic hysteria', his recurring nightmares of 'fantastic and terrible animals'. British doctor, Thomas Oliver, noted the 'extremely violent maniacal condition' of factory girls exposed to the chemical in the rubber trade in 1902. 'Some of them have become the victims of acute insanity, and in their frenzy have precipitated themselves from the top rooms of the factory to the ground.' It was under the Third Reich that the most severe cases of carbon disulphide poisoning were recorded. At the Widzewska Manufaktura cotton mill in Łódź, Poland, several workers were said to have become so ill they were sent to an asylum and never seen again. Pure carbon disulphide is colourless and said to smell sweet, but industrial carbon disulphide is yellow and smells like rotten radish. As I researched the chemical I found a photo taken through a microscope showing the effects of poisoning on the muscle, a close-up of swollen fibres and 'waxy degeneration' that resembled marbled fabric. I read about the disease's 'slow deceitful beginning', and its further symptoms of 'paraethesias, asthenia, difficulty in walking, mental deterioration, spastic paresis, alteration of speech'.

At Lenzing the women were woken at 3 a.m. for black bread and 'brown liquid', recalls Czech survivor Hanna Kohner. Her descriptions of camp life spare none of its depredations but pointillist details reveal the women's affinities. These 'walking skeletons' marched four kilometres from their Pettighofen barracks to the textile factory. They passed through 'the cobble-stoned village...along meadows, a dense forest and a small, clear stream'. Kohner doesn't describe many local people in her account (written with husband Walter). You have to imagine them in their gabled alpine houses, the red flowers like gashes in the window boxes. Or read the work of survivor Jean Améry, who spent his childhood nearby in the Gasthaus zur Stadt Prag. *The crimes of the regime entered my consciousness as collective deeds of the people.* Two weeks after aborting a baby in Auschwitz, Kohner is 'lucky' to work on the Lenzing drying machines. Others slaved without protection over vats of steaming carbon disulphide used to turn fir and beech into fabric for German army uniforms. The women worked twelve-hour days. Some were blinded by fumes and sores opened on their hands, others developed menstrual disorders from chemicals known to cause birth defects and degenerative brain disease. Many died and those who became ill or injured were gassed nearby at Mauthausen. They worked through the winter, marching through sleet and blizzards. At night, rain and snow through the barracks ceiling. Outbreaks of dysentery, tuberculosis and typhus. Hunger oedemas and skin disease from poor nutrition. The youngest among them was twelve. By March 1945 the women were starving. They picked roadside herbs on their way to the factory. They cooked snails in machine steam.

In a photograph from the United States Holocaust Memorial Museum, ten women stand outside the Pettighofen barracks. Some wear the striped jackets tied with rope sewn in the workshops of Dachau, Ravensbrück and Sachsenhausen. Isabel Wachenheimer, sixteen when she worked at Lenzing, wore a *KZ-Frauenjacke* of this kind. After her death in 2010, her jacket was found at her home in the Netherlands, wrapped in dry-cleaning plastic from the Rotterdam Hilton. I'm seized by these details – the plastic, which puts me in mind of a crime scene, the interval between young Isabel Maria of Germany and what transpired in that Rotterdam hotel. Most camp uniforms were destroyed after the war – they were stained, filthy, infested with lice or drenched in the DDT used for delousing after liberation. A man I know, a survivor who at ninety-nine continues to record the stories of others, lost his KZ jacket after his housekeeper took it to the drycleaners. Someone collected it by mistake, or perhaps it fell apart in a vat of perchloroethylene. In the Pettighofen photo only one woman looks young enough to be seventeen. She isn't tall. She stands at the back of the group, head angled up between the women's faces. I tell myself it can't be Renate, headed for solitude. She's too eager to be seen. Or perhaps I prefer to believe this than to imagine her waiting, after the war, to be found.

Among the 38,206 listed in the Mauthausen museum death book, are the nine women who died at Lenzing. Four of tuberculosis, intestinal obstruction and circulatory failure. I say died, but their injuries were sustained during their enslavement, and were, like the work itself, a slow murder. Five were crushed by a train on their way to the factory. Here's how Margaret Lehner recalls it in her oral account:

> [T]hey had to go there every day, early in the morning with their wooden shoes. And the winter was very strong. [...] And most of them didn't have any shoes, and they rolled paper around their toes and their feet. [...] And one day um, there is a local train, a small train from Atnang-Pucheim to Kammerschorsling [...] there was a bad accident [...] you have to cross the railway to the train before the train is coming, and five women didn't reach the other side [...] And we, we think the parts of the bodies are taken to Mauthausen, to the crematory of Mauthausen, because they are, there are no names within the books of the date, of the people who died here. And we think with no names.

There are no names within the books of the date. We think with no names. Lehner's faltering description of the unnamed women returns me to the Hollerith card on which Renate appears, in pieces, which is also how the Nazis referred to Jewish prisoners or labourers, using the word *Stück*. With some former prisoners Lehner organised a memorial to the women of Lenzing; she wanted 'to make the history still alive'.

What else is a ghost but a disturbance in the flow of time. More than once I've hovered over items in a chain store, until registering with a jolt that they're made from Lenzing fabric. Here, by a rack of flowing shirts in ecru, grey or mustard, under pitiless Zara halogens, I am haunted. The afterlife of state terror, genocide and slave labour erupts in such banal instances in everyday life; wholly private, practically invisible. It erupts in Lenzing's 'eco-fibre', *Edelweiss,* named after the woolly white alpine plant that symbolises the local people's purity. Edelweiss, which means 'noble' and 'white', was Hitler's favourite flower. It erupts as I scroll through photos of the Lenzing complex for signs of its history. Clinical foyer and conference rooms, tiled factory floor, logs stacked outside. It erupts while viewing a company promo spruiking green credentials, 'putting sustainability first...for the past 80 years' even as workers at their Indonesian factory wash toxic chemicals from viscose products into the Citarum River, one of the most polluted in the world. It erupts during Banc's tour of the Austrian factory, when he climbs the multi-level factory tower with a company rep who proudly notes there have been no suicides since 1950. Five years before that, Kohner watched the first liberators – a band of partisans looking like 'a chorus from an itinerant opera company' – approach the Lenzing camp. Schmidt and her fellow prison guards were preparing to flee. Schmidt seemed, writes Kohner, 'to have lost her iron German nerves. She seemed to choke on something. Her eyes became watery.' Her parting words before fleeing with Freinberger and Kunik, 'und macht uns keine Schande'. Don't bring dishonour to us. None of the women guards were ever brought to trial.

Years before I began searching in earnest, I found Renate's entry in the Yad Vashem database. She was mistakenly listed as having died in the Holocaust. I wrote to the museum asking them to correct the record, wondering, even then, if Renate would approve. Maybe she preferred to disappear. I thought then of Imre Kertész who once received, in a large brown envelope, the Buchenwald camp records in which his death was recorded. Kertész recalls this in his Nobel Prize speech. He says, 'I died once, so I could live', but cautions against thinking his story apocryphal. He doesn't want this to be an account of exceptionalism he says, accepting the literature prize. He prefers not to be singled out from the six million dead. What does it mean to search for a woman who so expressly chose to disappear, and to write her back into history? I recall Kertész's novel, *Kaddish for an Unborn Child,* in which survivor György Köves refuses to bring a child into a post-Holocaust world. Köves mourns this child that he won't conceive of, either literally or figuratively, and in the process grieves his own childhood cut short by deportation. Renate, it occurs to me, is equally inconceivable. If my attempt to bring her to life is both debt and guilt (in German the same word, *die Schuld*) it's also a way to resist a family story that turned her and her 'damage' into a warning about who could be assimilated and who could not.

Some time ago, an editor who read another work on this history advised against my approach. It isn't possible, she said, to combine epic historical events with smaller-scale contemporary material. War will always overshadow lives at peace, she seemed to say, or she was arguing for the Holocaust's exceptionalism. I didn't know how to explain that this shadowing was my very subject, and all the ways it threatened to obliterate me my deepest reason for writing. Only later did I see that prohibitions about representation can perpetuate the kinds of silence that took root in my mother, who'd passed to avoid the shame of being cast out and learned from the historic upheavals that splintered her family that major or minor feelings were comparatively inconsequential. This shadow remains with me still. It hangs about my writing as a ceaseless string of questions about which stories are mine to tell; what kinds of feeling are permissible;

how much of myself belongs in this account or ought to be sublimated; whether leaving myself out is wilful disappearance, distortion or erasure.

When Luc Tuymans painted Schwarzheide concentration camp it's said he had in mind a story about the prisoners there who tore their drawings into strips to keep them from being found. But Tuyman's long vertical lines, which seem to reference that tearing, in fact echo a drawing by inmate Alfred Kantor which contains the same wintry trees, the same black lines fencing the page. Painting what an inmate might have seen, writes Ulrich Loock, Tuymans 'takes the place of the inmate, to reproduce a substitute of something (trees) which he cannot reproduce (the concentration camp, death). The representation – hope-filled, fatal – of the other, who is oneself, is connected with the failure of the artist's own representation.' I recognise this failure in my attempts to recover Renate, *the other, who is oneself,* and how my acts of retrieval are similarly dependent on the accounts of others, partial, hope-filled.

I'll never know if it was Renate's wish to remain unknown – if she chose isolation or preferred to be recalled only as the young woman she was before Theresienstadt, Auschwitz, Lenzing and Mauthausen, the child who lived in Berlin with Hubert and Herta and sister Marion at Gustloffstrasse 17. It's only by reading Améry's sober work on exile that I can evoke Renate's experience. 'I rebel: against my past, against history...Nothing has healed.' Like most of my family, Améry didn't practice. In Salzkammergut he wore lederhosen and was raised as a Christian. He called himself a 'catastrophe Jew', an identity forced on him by the Nuremberg Laws. Reading Améry – *a person who could no longer say 'we'* – I have a sense of Renate's solitude. Améry can only say 'I' by force of habit. He says it without feeling in 'full possession' of himself. What's left of the self when it hasn't been held by family or friendship, by the machinery of the state? In her work on nostalgia, Svetlana Boym warns that 'the moment we try to repair longing with belonging, *the apprehension of loss with a rediscovery of identity*', we forfeit mutual understanding. Boym is thinking about exile and nationalism, but the same impulses spring up in a minor form within the family. Renate eventually received reparations under Germany's policy of *Wiedergutmachung* (making good again) but this didn't redeem life after liberation – as a maid in the Hotel Kinereth by the Red Sea; as an illiterate woman, married to an itinerant worker who beat her; estranged from what family remained across three continents. In Améry's 'analysis of resentments', in his experience of exile, he recognises the ongoingness of estrangement – not just from the new home and the old, but from the self.

I still have no picture of Renate, though I've recently received the reparations claim lodged by her grandmother Jenny Badrian in 1952. Somehow Jenny escaped the transport that sent her daughter and granddaughter to Auschwitz, remaining in Theresienstadt till liberation. By lodging the claim she took care of Renate – who was by then living precariously in Tel Aviv. Within this 340-page file (its extent unnoticed by me until exclamation marks arrived from the friend who helped me translate it), are reports from Renate's specialists, clinical descriptions of her *Lungentuberkulose*, her Neurosis Schizoider Psychopathy, her 'limited conceptual world'. After Theresienstadt, Auschwitz and Mauthausen, after years in the displaced persons camps on the Italian coast, after arriving, illegally, into a besieged Palestine in 1948, Renate was later hospitalised in Bat Yam, a psychiatric institution. A friend, deported from France with her mentally fragile mother to Israel in 1961, knows a little from her mother's later, itinerant years, about life on the edge in Tel Aviv. Bat Yam, she says, was colloquial for 'mad'. But it also means 'sea daughter'. After reading these reports, the family story of willed separation gains the elaborate tone of myth. What if psychological illness, not ambiguous 'damage' kept the family distant, and even threatened their assiduous assimilation? In an account that offers no insight into what a uniformed man might signify to a former maid in an SS barracks, Dr Erich Goldschlager, Specialist for Nervous and Mental Diseases, reports that Renate once assaulted an Israeli policeman. Did her madness – entirely rational in the face of what W.G. Sebald calls, 'the objective lunacy of history' – also make her unassimilable?

If my searching has partly been an attempt to provide what Gordon calls, 'a hospitable memory for ghosts *out of a concern for justice*', I must also admit that it's driven by a more personal, and possibly lifelong inquiry. What happens to the child whose temperament threatens the unspoken codes by which a family organises itself to survive? To belong to any group that forbids excess feeling is to relinquish genuine expression, mutual understanding. The ceaseless injury of being outcast can turn you into a detective, or a writer, who'll prefer almost any other mystery than one that confirms that outsider status. In the Hollywood redemption story, Renate has broken from the family that preferred not to acknowledge her madness, and how expressly it communicated her rage and grief. She chooses freedom over conformity, longing over belonging. Here she is, sluicing water down the halls of the Hotel Kinereth. Here she is, in a maid's uniform, zigaretten burning down as she stares across Tabariya,

which is the Palestinian name for the sea of Galilee, and is no sea at all, but a lake.

Goldschlager attributes Renate's trauma to the murder of her parents, to twelve years of persecution, to her lack of education and the violent husband she met in a displaced persons camp and divorced after a year. The doctor reports in German and his disparaging tone seeps through every machine translation. My Berlin friends, M and P, confirm this: 'a sloppiness pervades the commentary,' they tell me. 'There is a disdain, even scorn for Renate – the writer seems to find her appearance offensive – seems to take it personally that she's not attractive in a way he thinks appropriate, remarks on how her clothes are inadequate (nylon), she smells unwashed and has aged prematurely.' A few lines restore her humanity. She loved her dogs and learning languages. She smoked 20–40 a day, despite her tuberculosis. She carried into the doctor's rooms a primer used by schoolchildren from which she was teaching herself English. She had a passion for the cinema.

One day, searching archival images, I found a photo of women recuperating in the Mauthausen infirmary soon after liberation. Was Renate among them? The image is so overexposed that the wooden frames of the upper bunks look like windows full of sunlight. In the foreground a young woman, her face blurred and spectral from the long exposure. In every image from the camp I pick the most elusive figure and give her Renate's name. There's something unquantifiable in this photo, as if the whole scene were conjured by séance. But perhaps I only see it that way because the lives of women in the camps remain occluded, or because I want to fill in the spaces without distorting the picture. The blazing clerestory windows, the floating beds, the raw bulb in the foreground, the door at the far end of the hall opening onto nothing but glare. Somewhere beyond, camp brothels, once staffed by women from Ravensbrück. 'Now we belong to Mauthausen,' says a Hungarian survivor as she recalls their arrival from Auschwitz. In super-8 footage taken by the liberating army, she thanks the Americans with their k-rations of SPAM, powdered eggs, chocolate. 'They made from us people again,' she says in lilting, emphatic English. The infirmary photo is overexposed, a photographer friend tells me. Otherwise, with all that light from the windows, you wouldn't see the women at all.

Sources

Jean Améry, *At the Mind's Limits*, trans. Sidney and Stella Rosenfeld, Indiana University Press, 2009.

Edwin Black, *IBM and the Holocaust*, Crown Publishers, New York, 2001.

Paul David Blanc, *Fake Silk: The Lethal History of Viscose Rayon*, Yale University Press, 2016.

Lizou Fenyvesi, 'Reading Prisoner Uniforms: The Concentration Camp Prisoner Uniform as a Primary Source for Historical Research', *Textile Society of America Symposium Proceedings*, 2006.

Avery Gordon, 'Some Thoughts on Haunting and Futurity', *Borderlands*, Vol. 10, No. 2, 2011.

Imre Kertész, 'Heureka!', Nobel Speech in *Nobel Lectures*, Melbourne University Press, 2006.

Imre Kertész, *Kaddish for an Unborn Child*, trans. Tim Wilkinson, Vintage, 1990.

Hanna and Walter Kohner, Frederick Kohner, *Hanna and Walter: A Love Story*, iUniverse, 2008.

Interview with Margaret Lehner and Yehuda Bauer, United States Holocaust Museum, 1994.

Ulrich Loock, in *Luc Tuymans*, Phaidon, London, 1996.

W.G. Sebald, *Campo Santo*, trans. Anthea Bell, Penguin, London, 2006.
Magdalena Zolkos, 'Resentment, Trauma Subjectivity and the Ordering of Time', *Reconciling Community and Subjective Life: Trauma Testimony as Political Theorizing in the Work of Jean Améry and Imre Kertész*, Bloomsbury, NY, 2010.

My gratitude to Michelle Moo, to Priya Basil and Matti Fredrich-Auf der Horst, Josiane Behmoiras, Saskia Beudel, Gail Jones, Phillip Maisel, Karen O'Connell and Maria Tumarkin.

Image pp 26–27
Survivors in the women's barracks at the newly liberated lower camp of Mauthausen, United States Holocaust Memorial Museum Photo Archives #38063, Courtesy of Ray Buch, Copyright of United States Holocaust Memorial Museum.

JOSEPHINE ROWE
SPECIAL STUFF

Josephine Rowe is the author of three story collections and a novel, *A Loving, Faithful Animal*. Her story collection *Here Until August* was shortlisted for the 2020 Stella Prize. She is currently in residence at the Dorothy and Lewis B. Cullman Centre at the New York Public Library, researching a new novel.

IT WAS MY TURN TO HOLD HER. I wrapped her in the special stuff. Then he wrapped us both in the special stuff, leaving a corner untucked to fold himself into. He still had the windows to seal over. We waited in the deepest part of the house and hoped that the light, when it came, might not reach us. (We imagined there would be light.) She slept and I shivered, though it was not cold, was almost never cold now. Through the untucked fold I could see part of the front wall, and his shadow thrown hectic across it. Rip of tape as he worked to mask the glass. Then no more shadow.

Are you coming? I mouthed into the dark. Not wanting to wake her. I'm not sure he heard but there he was, at last, moving with the usual composure but sweating a new panic smell. He tucked himself into what was left, which we both knew was not enough. I suspected that none of it was really enough, that we were just going through the motions now. Living out the statutory rising inflection, the hopeful key change at the end of the grim newscast, the kind that makes a flimsy play for salvation but offers no clear avenue towards it. I'd laughed at enough of those old pamphlets – turtles in helmets, bears under tables. But here we were.

Special or not, I didn't like the feel of the stuff on my skin. Neither of us did, the baby and me. They called it 'intelligent' and that's almost what it felt like – sentient and clingy.

There're worse feelings, he murmured into my hair, and we stood quiet for a while and waited to know about them.

Officials assured they'd localised the event to a 60-km radius, a seventeen-hour window. Detractors and conspiracy theorists called bunk – who knew what scale of administrative atrocities could be carried out over that range, over seventeen hours, with no witnesses? We were within the projected hot zone. Towards the outer edge of the hot zone, in the greenish-yellow. But there was a lot of room for error, and anyway no time and no means to get elsewhere. Our friends in the green zones sent us care packages, lavish hampers. The sentiments were ambiguous, but there hadn't been this much booze in the house since we were married.

We'd fasted for the better part of the week before, so that our bodies would expect less of us. Riding out the caffeine headaches and the snarkiness, the shitty name-calling, the baby's wails, the booze withdrawals and the too-vivid dreams that only made us want to reach again for something, anything to blur the edges.

The night before we had a sort of dress rehearsal, almost like pitching a new tent in the backyard ahead of setting out for the wilds. Similar air of excitement. Only then it became obvious that we hadn't ordered enough of the stuff. I didn't think of us as especially large people. Though there are countries we've visited where we had to sleep diagonally across the beds, so I suppose in a global sense we were. Are. Bigger than average. Anyway, the stuff was really just surface cover, skin protection; no defence against respiratory complications or anything more stealthy. Not like we could live here, swaddled up, indefinitely. Anyway, it was too late to order more, unless you wanted to trawl the black market; authorised supplies had run dry within hours.

There was the choice of standing up or lying down. He put on a sort of Dodge City gunslinger drawl: Are we gonna take it standing up or lying down? We tried it both ways. Lying down was more comfortable but once you were down you were down for the duration, down for the count. Standing up you had less chance of becoming trapped, could shuffle around a bit if needed, a choreographed lumbering like the haunted inanimate objects in cartoons, or kids in outsized foam costumes in Christmas pageants.

We chose to take it standing up. We were equipped with water, juice in little foil pouches, like astronaut provisions. Besides the pouches of water and juice, there were snacks that were nourishing but uniformly unappealing, to discourage panic eating. A small tin of xylitol ginger chews for anxious stomachs, although even these had an unpleasant aftertaste, a bitterness I figured had been added especially, as a deterrent. A tube of medicinal lip balm. Caffeine tablets for fatigue, magnesium tablets for muscle cramps, a natural antihistamine to encourage infant drowsiness. The mood stabilisers he's been on for twenty years, since before I knew him. (You wouldn't want to know me without them, he's said, again and again, but that theory remains untested.) Other pills, vacuum-sealed and wrapped fifteen or twenty times around with plastic film, so that we wouldn't mistake them. But we weren't going to think anymore about those unless forced to. Baby things, so many baby things. Our two fully charged phones, twenty-three hours of life between them. This was comforting, somehow, their combined battery amounting to greater than the window of catastrophe. Or the theoretical window of possible catastrophe. Though nobody could say what would happen with the towers. Already the signal had become patchy, and the birds had been growing quieter, retreating with – and in spite of – each lengthening day.

We tried to tell the right stories in there, hopeful stories: everything we've ever won, days we would like to relive, to invite the other back to, the way other people do with family properties, lake houses and such – notches on the doorframe, trees planted to mark a birth that now bestowed shade and fruit, heirloom pluots ripening on a windowsill...We had none of that, nothing like that. He and I had grown up very differently, though it didn't figure all that much because each of our pasts had been neatly swept up behind us. We each could have rewritten our histories from scratch and there'd be no one, not a sibling or any other soul to rat us out, to say it hadn't happened that way or that we were leaving out some critical, humiliating detail. Of course I left things out. I'm certain he did, too. But I was – we were, I think – mostly honest.

We had agreed not to count the hours. I tried to stand in such a way that the stuff wasn't touching any exposed skin but it was impossible.

I could sense his own agitation, but he spoke in the measured, wilfully optimistic tones of CBT worksheets. Tell me, he said, what would you rather be feeling?

It was his lot, even in normal times, to comfort me, and if I resented this (yes) he never seemed to.

When I didn't answer right away he pressed, Come on. Something from before you knew me.

I'm thinking, I said.

I tried to take us there. Somewhere distantly bucolic, outmoded, tactile. A river still safe for swimming, the gentle trawl of its current around shins, cool soft clay underfoot, the continual chirr of yabbies beneath the surface. Or plunging limbs down into stores of sun-warmed grain – wheat, barley, rye – which was strictly forbidden due to hygiene. And punishable by something long forgotten to me now, or perhaps threatened but never actually carried out, because I was already a burdened child and my grandparents were softhearted, and their small farm nearly bust, anyway.

Besides, who could help themselves, when small enough to be wholly submerged, to be held, secure, at all possible points of touch? Easing into the storage containers as you would a brimming bathtub, trying not to overflow, to splash the grain over the side and give yourself away.

It gave you away anyway. Grain in your clothes and hair, your underwear, in the whorl of an ear. You even wanted to plunge your head under but you didn't. Or you did once and then never again, learning your lesson; chaff rasping at your tonsils for days after, reddening your corneas, forming grit in your tear ducts.

My throat felt parched from remembering. The wheat dust, the chaff-filled air. He held a sachet of electrolyte mix to my lips and I took a mouthful, my shoulder already aching from the baby's sling. My arms aching from easing the weight off my shoulder. There was no room to put her down, or even to hand her over, without briefly exposing ourselves. He braced my arms with his, our breath close. Hot in there, in the shared air. We got into a familiar rhythm, sharing it. Like at the start of things: me lying flat on top of him, our lips around the same breath, passing it lungs to lungs, waiting to go faint. Somebody would tap, lightheaded, break away. Then the glorious oxygen hit, all the bright rushing in and the sex we spent it on, our inhibitions starved away.

I'd never wanted to inhale another person so deeply, absolutely.

Learning that there were evolutionary, immunological causes for this only sharpened the hungering.

We had agreed: not to count the hours, not to run down the time on our phones. We went through the games we played as kids, before the internet, bored in back seats or rained-out weekenders. Through the times we thought the world would end, or at least our stakes in it, before righting ourselves: back to the hopeful and harmless stories, pressing each other for the right details – what was the dog's name, and how tall the trees, were you always so...? Aware we were as much passing these stories down to ourselves, with each retelling, the ancestors of incident that now stood for what, exactly? What, after all, did we still mean to make known to one another?

When he was young he had premonitions, prophetic dreams, but they were so prosaic he was embarrassed to share them. He'd never told me this before.

I never told anyone, he said. I thought their boringness meant I was deficient in some way, deficient in imagination.

He said he never saw any useful shit coming.

(I did not say: Obviously, case in point – you didn't see this. But maybe he had and just hadn't let on, hadn't wanted to spook me.)

I asked him, what was there, then?

Mostly it would just be the numbers and the colours of things, but no lucky numbers and no lucky colours.

My mother would have found a way, I said. Could you pick horses?

I never tried, he said. Horses never came up.

My mother would've had me picking horses. She had me do

that anyway, kind of a way of getting me involved. Like bonding? Even though I'm not exactly mystical. At least she had someone to blame when they didn't place.

Were you any good...at choosing horses?

No, hopeless. That's why she packed me off to the farm. (It wasn't why, but decades on I still needed to joke about it, to laugh it off, have been laughing it off incrementally for decades. He missed that cue, though, and went on.)

Anyway, he said – and I knew that if there had been just a bit more elbow room he would have made a little sweeping motion with his hand – Anyway, it was nothing exploitable, nothing you could commodify. More like that the milk would be bad even though the use-by was fine. Or that the second birch from the right would come down in the next storm even though there was nothing outwardly wrong with it. Beetles, it turned out. Whoomph. Down it came.

After a certain age, he said, I stopped paying attention. Or, I stopped being able to differentiate. Maybe whatever it was – the signal? – got scrambled with the internet. Or puberty. Since the late nineties there's just been a kind of...residue.

A residue, I repeated.

Like, an aura of recognition? Around certain things.

So, like deja vu, I said disappointed.

No, he said, defensive now. Stickier than that.

We stood in a clammy silence.

You're disappointed, he said.

Why would I be disappointed, I said, and let the silence flood back.

He reached for his phone, out of habit I suppose. Even though we had agreed.

In the screenlight his face was damp and crumpled, irradiant, like a new moth's wing.

What are you looking for, I asked?

There's no signal at all now, he said. He patted me down for mine, switched it on, though of course we were on the same plan, the same network. The baby, little lightning rod that she is, was beginning to rouse and fret.

Since it's on, could you play her the song?

The song was a gentle Appalachian folk number that was almost certainly a murder ballad. But it was the baby's clear favourite and who were we to judge. No darker than most nursery rhymes; far better than autotune. It was a song about sparrows, the singer drawing on the hymnals of his childhood, on the Gospel of Luke, that had not, in the end, restored him to much faith.

We let it play through a couple of times, then switched the phones back off.

Neither of us said the obvious; that it would be easier without the baby, that the baby was poorly timed. But the thought was large in there with the three of us. Without the baby there would be less to fear, less to fear for. We had convinced ourselves, some part of ourselves, that the world might yet become a less precarious place in the years after her birth, that she might inherit a tenable future. This, too, was probably biology at work. It vanished in the instant she took air. Her hair and baby teeth yet to emerge and already laced with plastics and pollutants, the long half-life of detonations that had occurred far away and long before her lifetime, even before mine.

It must've been falling dark by then. All the hours upright playing hell on my knees, my pelvic floor. I said I wished it would hurry up and hit so I could piss. We imagined there would be some sign. Fierce light. Seismic activity, at least some noise. In truth the birds had been quieting for much longer, only so gradually that it was difficult to prove, however obvious it seemed to most.

A wind was up, outside, the kind with a voice of its own, that gives forum to the trees. Then there was another voice, very human and plaintive, and a dull pounding at the door.

The pounding came harder, and the voice.

Did you see this, I whispered, hissed. Though to be fair we had both seen this: some late convert to dread, fatally unprepared, now freaked by the signal outage and the wind and whatever else.

The effects would be immediate, I was sure, near enough to painless. Or would they be? A small, alright a not insignificant part of me was curious to see how the skeptics, the non-compliers fared, so the rest of us could know whether it was worth all the trouble, the expense. But then my mind would scroll through the usual disaster archives, historical poster victims canonised by the international press, and I discovered there was still room enough, in our airless synthetic cocoon, to be ashamed.

We waited for the splintering of the lock, or the shattering of glass, for the paving stones from the front yard to crash through the front windows. To be exposed, to whatever was coming. The knocking – the person or persons – went around the house a couple of times, rattling and banging. Then at last they gave up and went away.

It might've been Leise, I said, after it had been quiet a while.

It wasn't, he said, flatly.

Because she was kind of on the fence about it all. If it was Leise I feel bad, a bad neighbour.

Don't, he said.

You know for sure?

It just didn't sound like Leise.

Panic – it does weird things to the vocal folds, the pitch.

I'm aware of that, he said. (His own voice seemed to have dropped a register.)

We listened. Only wind.

What about after this? I asked

How do you mean?

You said you couldn't differentiate; that doesn't mean they don't come, anymore. The visions, or the stickiness, whatever.

He was making it up, probably, or drawing on old stock to console me, yet again. I might've seen that if I'd been in a more receptive state, paying attention to how analogue it all was. Animals and trees, patterns of weather. Augural stuff. How clear the skies – alignments of planets, stars, celestial arcs suddenly made visible to the naked eye. It began with the birds coming back. With clear waterways and the proliferation of sentient plant life.

The baby wasn't in any of it. None of us were.

While he spoke I hummed the sparrows song into the top of her head (her feathery hair) which smelled as always: divine. No hint of distress from her. Maybe she liked it in there, in the close, the dark, like a return to the womb but with larger company. (Notches on the doorjamb, benevolent creaturely faces found in the wood grain. Sitting quietly on plastic lawn chairs at dusk, waiting for the bandicoots to emerge from their burrows at the edge of the property, their stripes just visible... Did we do that, my grandparents and me, or did I invent this? The songs of birds I used to wake with, whose music she might not ever learn.)

After a while I stopped humming the melody, settling on a single, sustained note, the same I've used to self-soothe since I was small. I'm not really musical. I don't know which note it is, or any science around it; only that I found it when I was young and it works, has always worked, in the way I imagine purring does. Maybe there's a different note for everyone, a particular frequency that accords with their dimensions and DNA. Or it could just as easily be the same note, for all of us, a deep common resonance we are at the brink of forgetting, but which some part of us never fails to recognise, to harken to.

The knocking came again, depleted, but persistent.

It has to be someone good, I whispered. Someone halfway decent, or they'd have gone ahead and bricked the windows by now.

It doesn't matter, he said, it's not like we have anything to spare.

But he mustn't have liked the way that sounded out loud. We'd spoken of it, many times over the years, how we just wanted to come through the worst of things without doing anything we might be ashamed of afterwards. Or not acting, when called upon to act.

The knocking went on, at longer intervals. He began filling my pockets with the contents of his own, then slipped his phone into my free hand and squeezed my fingers.

I'll go and explain, he said. I'll just go and explain that to them, that there's nothing we can...Let us not – he was searching for something – Let us not lose our...

He didn't finish. Couldn't find the word, or couldn't say it. Carefully he unwrapped himself and moved towards the sound, away from us.

There was the door, then the wind calling through the house, room to room. And the desire, even now, to play my fingers through it.

SARAH HOLLAND-BATT
FIVE POEMS

Sarah Holland-Batt is the author of two poetry volumes, *Aria* and *The Hazards,* which received the Prime Minister's Literary Award for Poetry in 2016, and a book of essays on contemporary poetry, *Fishing for Lightning: The Spark of Poetry.* Her third book of poems, *The Jaguar,* is forthcoming in May.

Pikes Peak

Hiking near the timberline at twelve thousand feet
my father mistakes an almost silent stroke for vertigo—
immobilisation that arrives like a tsunami,
the body withdrawing to its furthest reaches,
brain stem stoppered for a paralysing second.
He sits winded in a rubble of rose granite
staring at the infinite regression of quaking aspen,
valley after valley to the horizon,
stunned by his own elevation. Then fear,
comprehension: he has lost the language
for water, aspirin. An icy breeze shearing
off snow, heads of spruce and bristlecone
stretching all the way down to the switchback
roads where motorcycles lean in terminal arcs.
At this height everything grows deformed
by wind and cold—flag trees with a single comb
of greenery down a leeward side,
krummholz pines twisted into pretzel bends,
scratchings of alpine parsley, dwarf clover.
Who knows exactly when it started or was over—
a lightning storm in the skull, its barometer
registering no drop in pressure—then whole zones
denuded like the palms after Castle Bravo—
detonation raising storeys of ocean to the sky.
I gave myself a fright, he says, and shakes his head—
a bull shifting a cloud of horseflies.
Around my father tundra grass is blowing
grain by stunted grain. This is the vista

about which Katharine Lee Bates wrote 'America
the Beautiful'—the only line of which I ever remember
is *O beautiful for pilgrim feet*, which to me
means precisely zero. But if I strain I can still see him
sitting dumbfounded in that field of feldspar,
his beautiful pilgrim feet laced into white Reeboks and gym socks
as a sunburst ripples through his brain.
My father is calm as a monk whose long meditation
produces imperceptible shifts
in his physiognomy, and I understand my father
went up the mountain for the same reason
everyone goes up mountains.
He went up the mountain to change.

Neurostimulator

The transhuman future
arrives for my father
as a matchbox purring in his chest—
battery pack biohacking
his brain, titanium ingot
shrink-wrapped in skin.

A whisp of silver cable
running up his spine is visible
only in silhouette
when he turns his neck—
subcutaneous ripple
threaded to his cortex.

After the surgery
his forehead bears a buckled scar—
a runnel ringing his crown
like the trace of Roman fortifications
on a bald hillside, a ghost yarmulke.

Underneath, a confetti
of microelectrodes receives pulses
from his chest, urging
his neurons: connect.

But the man who always
adored machine logic
resents being programmed.

He blames the box
for each misjudged step:
his faltering, arrhythmic gait,
all signs of rebel code.

He only learns later
about the risks of malware—
his firewall is vulnerable,
any minute his microchip
could be hacked,
he could be made to moonwalk,
sent haywire, surveilled.

They say the server is secure
but there's no way to be sure.
My father's face unreadable
stone as he insists
his mind is his and his alone.

The Night Shift

Like hummingbirds attending
to injections of nectar

nurses squeak from room to room
in white sneakers. Buzzers

zip and sting like electric
whipbirds. My mother presses

David Attenborough to her ear—
his voice eases through the plastic

receiver. A caiman floats
in the Pantanal's scum green,

a crown of orange butterflies
sipping tears from its eye's skin. Salt

crystals sugaring each wingbeat.
Her chemotherapy drips. Night

cinches its tendrils around
blinking fluorescents—

light that will not die.
My mother drifts in and out

of a sleep that never
settles, but rises and dips

and rises. She's bone tired. The eye
of the caiman opens and closes—

slick membrane clinging
to never-ending saltlick. It's unclear

if it feels the infinitesimal weight lift
when each butterfly takes flight.

Vital Signs

Nurses flank my mother like bridesmaids
in lavender gowns and gloves.

One wheels a lavender trash can
beside her bed—coded reliquary

for her toxic body.
Poison pulses above my mother's head,

a sluggish bladder
coffined in a violet sleeve,

a diaphanous chrysalis
too hazardous to touch.

The clipboard where nurses jot
vitals, urine and bloods

is the colour of the jacaranda tree
blossoming outside

because it is November, season of trampled
purple on the cricket field

behind the hospital where children
bat in match-day whites—

a roasting wind driving ash
and burnt grass into their lungs,

red leather cracking
like dry thunder on willow,

the air everywhere glazed with smoke
from distant fires making themselves known.

Brazil

My mother and I eat takeout: crispy basil prawn and red duck curry. Last week in his nursing home, my father told my mother he was taking her to Brazil. He'd been thinking about where to go for a long time, he said, and landed on Brazil. Its borders touch ten countries, he said, which is convenient. How long are we going for? my mother asked. At least a year, he said. Will we see the Amazon? my mother asked. Oh yes. And Sarah? my mother asked. She'll have to come, my father said. I don't know if she can, my mother said, she has to work. Her work will understand, my father said. I taste lychee and chilli. My mother sips her wine. We're going first class, my father said. We've been married for fifty years, and you deserve it. Then he burst into tears. My mother spoons curry over coconut rice as she tells me this. The rice is rich and sweet. I just thanked him, she said. I knew he'd forget all about it. But my father didn't forget. The next day, he said he'd been running the numbers, and he wasn't sure whether he could afford to go to Brazil first class, but we would definitely go business. And I see it, I see my father at 40,000 feet, I see him craning his neck to look out of the window, I see him flying over Mato Grosso do Sul, I see him flying like a distant god over cerrado savannah and the snaking wetlands of the Pantanal, I see my father touching the corner of his mouth with a linen napkin as the plane begins its descent, its wings flexing, I see the silverwear gleaming in front of him, I see him lifting a cup filled with jaguar's blood up to the light, how it gleams like wine, I see the raw jaguar's heart filleted in the finest slivers, carmine red, laid out like a stinking meat flower on the plate in front of him.

The Parachute

All night my father hangs upside down
in the hospital basement
trapped under the huge pulsing bell
of a crystal jellyfish. He is buckled there—
snaps of metal crisscross his thorax, a tangle
of suspension lines skein around his legs.
Ripstop nylon blooms and shrinks above him—
canopy of army green, a fever skin.
He cannot understand how he landed behind enemy lines
in this crawlspace, this jumble of copper pipes
and surplus gear. He moves slow as an insect in agar.
His eyes are blind and shine with effort.
His rig is snagged on some unseen obstacle—
a tree, or the intimation of a tree.
His fatigues he recognises, but the parachute
is his father's—the one that failed to deploy
when his Hawker Hurricane was shot down
over France, and there's a plastic strap noosed
around his wrist he can't undo. He is in for observation,
or is it reconnaissance—the mission keeps moving—
but if he cranes his neck he can glimpse
a keyhole opening in the fabric above his head:
a clear pupil, the apex vent, portal
to a world he might see through to
if only he could reach it, if only he wasn't
plummeting further with every breath.

BRIAN CASTRO
BRIEF LIVES

...people are invisibly connected without knowing it, they touch one another through lives that to them remain forever foreign, they step into times which they think are not theirs, they walk through landscapes which are new only to them but which have existed for centuries.

Daša Drndić, *Belladonna*

Brian Castro is the author of the prize-winning Australian classic *Shanghai Dancing*, and recipient of the 2014 Patrick White Award. His novels include *The Garden Book* and *The Bath Fugues*, both shortlisted for the Miles Franklin Literary Award. His most recent work, *Blindness and Rage*, won the 2018 Prime Minister's Literary Award for Poetry.

JOHN AUBREY ONCE SAID: 'It's a war between men and women. It's not about Joan of Arc.' He continued, 'and anyway, beneath all that armor she had balls.' Maybe it wasn't Aubrey, but it sure as hell sounded like he would have said it. Given that he did or didn't say it, who was Aubrey? He lived through the sacking of Oxford University; the English Civil War; the Great Fire of London. He was good at observation but was blindly swindled by a woman he wanted to marry. He had witnessed urban conflagrations but he would never have seen a bushfire. He would have liked the guesthouse to which they all retreated now, here in South Australia, because it was the only open country without too many trees and was surrounded by acres of vines, though those were being singed at the edges. People drove their cars up and pointed the bonnets at the ridge of fire. If the smoke became too thick they knew they had to get out in that same direction and then turn left or right, making sure they weren't trying to outrun the fire coming from behind. It was a nice guesthouse although the people already gathered there did not seem to know one another, but they had all stayed there at one time or other because they all remembered that they were supplied with Japanese kimonos and that their bathrooms had thick glass on three sides which looked out at the vineyards and the hills beyond, without fearing for their own privacy or modesty. Perhaps that is what connected them: grapevines and nakedness.

Someone was speaking in the large lounge room and the others had pulled up chairs and ottomans – *it's a deep trawl*, he said, *I'd rather forget my childhood*. He looked unhappy, like all the pictures of Tolstoy, a long white beard, never smiling because of missing front teeth. Since September his father had been dangerously ill. *The old are dispensable for those who never knew them well.* The speaker had been incarcerated in a junior boarding school from the age of five, then to big school and then college. His father had been a QC, who viciously prosecuted anyone below the rank of an Eastern Suburbs property developer. *It is the waiting that I do best. For nothing most of the time. I spend my days restoring things.* He said it as if the world needed to be put right. *Once something is really broken, it is almost impossible to mend it. Only if it is worn out, can you bring it to a state of possibility.* He said his wife was worn out but not broken. Where is she? She is at home, refusing to leave even though the fire was starting to ring the property. *You cannot force a person to leave their home. It is against the law.* He is very worried and concerned for her safety, he said. They had made a pact. They put it in writing in case of repercussions. She would not leave. He had spent thousands of dollars to protect their place against fires...pumps, hoses on the roofs, multiple water tanks, mature camellias. She would be safe. He and his wife did not speak to each other except on very rare occasions. His wife said he had dementia, though he didn't really believe that was the cause of their silences. He also said places, like families, were often fatal.

There was a kind of shuffling about. People looked uneasy, as though a crime were about to be committed. Somebody coughed as sirens sounded in the distance, then an old woman who looked as though she had been asleep, her head back and her mouth open, took up the skein of talk like a trout after a fly. He was always so neat, she said. Everything about him was thought through until it became second nature: good habits, cleanliness, always smelling of Pears soap – kind of rubbery and unperfumed – and since he was a doctor, these things went down well with his patients. Then he retired and he started to plan things well in advance, like buying a shipping container and burying it on our property, which I hated...we had countless arguments over that...and he began pouring concrete steps, positioning corrugated steel sheeting across the roof, planting grass on top. We argued over everything, which was something we had never done before when he was at the surgery, when he was happy as a child in a sandpit, until a medical conglomerate turned his practice into a multi-purpose clinic. Now he had to make himself busy, not only because he thought the Chinese were coming, yes, they were going to take over the world, but with some ventilation the bunker would be handy in a bushfire and it doubled up as a wine cellar, being very cold in there, especially in the winter. In summer he put our ski clothing in the steel lockers he'd bought because ski clothing was expensive as were our trips to the South Island in New Zealand where in Queenstown even the street signs were in Japanese, which alarmed him because he had imagined a kind of Nordic holiday without all those Asians on the slopes chattering in a language he couldn't understand. Then abruptly we stopped taking overseas trips, so he moved the ski clothing from the bunker to make room for his Grange wines, which he purchased at auction, sometimes topping out at $500 a bottle. He was very proud of that collection, though we never drank any of it, when after a couple of years he discovered that silverfish had bred in the darkness and had eaten all the labels since they must have liked the glue or the taste of the paper, so he didn't know what year each vintage was and that was when he had his heart attack, stumbling up the steps gasping for air. I don't regret having argued so much with him; if only he had let the sunshine in we could have had a lovely old age. I've never gone back down into that bunker. I thought of making it my studio and doing some sculpting but there was only artificial, fluorescent light. I don't even know what's in there now; snakes perhaps. Nobody's touched the wine since, until I had my gardener put the cases into the boot of my car upon my evacuation.

The portrait painter, who had been unnoticed in the corner of the vast lounge room looked up from his cedar cigar box lid and like many painters, spoke briefly: If life is short and art is long, then the corollary would be to do short art and live a long life. Art kills as much as snakes. But we could all do with some wine.

Who the hell was this old guy sitting in the corner, prolix as a sphinx? He never spoke again that night. He was unhoused. To speak through thought was to make others wary. He could sense this and occupied himself with his panel, which nobody wanted to view; indeed, nobody wanted to approach him and he gradually faded into the dark as the generator was turned on, dim lights contrasting with the reddening sky. Perhaps he was painting by smell.

Jack didn't see the point of eating vegetables because he said his wife Marge only made vegetables and though he was convinced that veges were more healthy for them, he could not feel any appetite eating them, raw or cooked and at times read Claude Lévi-Strauss to try to make sense of this whole cooking and eating thing, but thought it better if he drank a lot of wine beforehand and could then say nice things about Marge's cooking, but mostly he snuck down to the mall and had hamburgers and when he felt particularly Jewish, as he was, ordered pastrami and pickles New York style and came home saying he was not really hungry, but he always helped her cook vegetables, calling her his beloved Margarine and suggested they start a garden of greens because he liked cos lettuce and would eat that and horse radish like a horse, going yum yum, just to please her. Now he said to the room full of people that he had floaters in his eyes, not pie floaters but all kinds of three-dimensional shapes shifting like holograms and these geometries were populating his sight. He was not wishing to complain of his numerous and various eye operations, but said he could live with the imagination of them, addressing the painter, who did not look up from his work, that he could understand exactly what Maurits Cornelis Escher was driving at with mathematical inspiration, revolving three-dimensional figures right there in the cornea, which was Escher's middle name, at the same time saying with all the veges Marge ate it didn't do her any good since she had bowel cancer and had died in his arms, as he said, *exploding* there in his arms, and he had her contact lens cases, all pristine, for anyone who wore contacts and needed them. *Gratis*.

Not being a performer...in answer to introducing himself, the old Chinese man with a large white moustache who came in late on a bicycle and who raised chickens only for their eggs which he sold by the roadside, neglected to finish his response... but had he done so would have said you could put anything in the mouths of performers, even poison, which would fill the air, as would the sound of applause. So he sat there smiling and twiddling his thumbs. John Aubrey would have called him a *scobberlotcher*, though he worked part-time at the local cemetery and kept flowers on graves that were neglected...cherry blossoms mostly, which he grew with great care. Aubrey, being an antiquarian, liked digging up old bones, along with Sir Thomas Browne, but the English climate mostly discouraged cherry blossoms, which needed to be grown alternatively in full sun, in partial or mostly warm shady areas with deep, fertile soil. In

Uraidla, South Australia, the *gardien de cimetière* was thinking of a rhyme: *those who harbour desire were prone to the storm of satire*. In season. He could have posted this as a flyer at the cemetery gates but decided that being a postman and a grave-keeper seemed almost diametrically opposed; for one thing, he found it difficult chiselling into stone. But letter-writing was also an engraving, *gravitas*, a silent, dignified marker. So the silence of the painter and the grave-keeper's finger-miming found something in common, though it was not immediate to the eye. Not like a painting of yews anyway.

When he was a young man, the still-handsome vigneron Peter was saying (he's in his seventies now), he had broken up with his girlfriend who had turned reckless. She climbed outside the railing under the atrium of a shopping mall and fell, and though she had no intention of jumping, she was careless nevertheless and there she was, still conscious upon the mosaiç floor, moving her hands as if imploring him to help and he ran down the stairs struggling past screaming shoppers, lost in a labyrinth of arcades and escalators, the crowd rushing in one direction to gape, and he was kneeling over her, still looking on helplessly, taking her hand, afraid to do anything else in case of aggravating an internal injury. Years later, crippled and sarcastic, she moved her hands in the same way as if imploring him, not for help anymore but to mock him for his inaction which was the same inaction that was an avoidance that time he revisited the shopping mall and there she was in a wheelchair selling badges for some charity and he melted into the crowd pretending he didn't see her. He could have told her that whatever he did, whether outdoor work or indoor reading about vines, the bruising of grapes or soil drainage, there was always a high degree of desperation: sirens in his head, the heavy sound of wings, time's osculation. He said to his current wife, the old lady dozing next to him on the sofa, that once something is broken, it is impossible to mend it. Only if it is worn out, can one bring it to a state of possibility. The fires may have destroyed fifty years of hard work, he said.

People who have done time, I notice, always stand out from the others. People who have done time won't look you in the eye, instead they are second-guessing you, figuring out whether you are picking up their trail. People who have done time know how long it takes to understand the nature of time; they mark time, kill time, spend time. Maybe the artist had done time; maybe the grave-keeper; maybe even the vigneron, who goaded his girlfriend over the rail, seeing how far she would go. Everyone is connected here through their vignettes, like tendrils of the vine, since all they could do now was to wait together and they would have to do their best, finger-drumming, foot-tapping, compressing their lives, connected, but unable to move forward.

The grave-keeper said there was a kind of mushroom which fed off the nitrogen released from a dead body. It marked the graves which were freshly putrefying. He was fond of oxymorons, parataxes and taxonomies. He called the mushrooms 'corpse-finders of the recently lost' or that they were 'the cloakroom of cadavers' or that they had 'truffles of their own'. Mushrooms guided him when he forgot temporary markers or had misplaced gravestones.

The guitarist, who had long hair and who now felt confident enough to speak in older company, said he had to leave his guitars behind at his house, and that they were probably all burnt. He looked very sad and wanted to say that chords on a guitar were like tendons, knotted together like catgut, taking you to places known and unknown, depending on their progression; feline feelings of comfort and exploration, housed and unhoused. Of course he couldn't put any of this into words, because words were not what a musician could use. Like the fact that when his then father-in-law gave him for his birthday a Luger pistol captured from a German officer in the Second World War, the guitarist couldn't bring himself to say thanks because he was leaving his wife. So he placed the pistol wrapped in an oilcloth inside a Tupperware box, sealed it and buried it under the house. It was the era in which there was an amnesty, in which people had to turn in unlicensed guns and he wasn't going to do it because he did not trust the cops, who would question him like a drug dealer, since he had long hair and looked suspicious.

One thing that jailbirds know: one gets deepened by doing time. Not refined deepening but rough deepening. You just know what is surface on people. But there's not a lot of excavation after that. Class is all skating on thin ice. The real depth is in life knowing death. Not many know that even when they're dying, that all their life is surface and presumed depth, even if they read, even if they had presumed to have acquired culture, even if they listened to classical music or went to the ballet or the opera. It's what the Nazis missed: that they missed deep time through efficiency. Their thoroughness and completeness was their goal. Which forever condemned them. Their Bavarian Catholic mysticism and brutal, petulant fantasy. I understand waste, the guitarist could have said. But that doesn't mean I don't have the same subjectivity of being the best of the best, which I will never achieve in this life. Better not to have this aim. Better to let things flow through feeling without interpretation, without a sieve, outside of oneself but inside as well, without knowing or saying. Which of course, guaranteed mediocrity.

The gathering was taken aback. How strange, being taken aback. Many of the old ladies were frightened by this talk, as if the musician with his long hair were a Raskolnikov, though of course they did not know his name, that somehow he was murderous. If only he would have a guitar to play and not talk. Of course he would hate charwomen and only play to Czarinas. But here they were, all intrigued like Czarinas.

I sit here not wanting to speak because to speak is in a way to show off something and I have nothing to show these days, I say to myself with alarming intimacy because I say it half-aloud, and some people in the room may have heard me, but no one spoke, perhaps out of politeness, or fear of being rebuked by a man who looked like Confucius. *Some people shut down when they retire,* said an acquaintance who once came up to my hotel room in Barcelona and I was embarrassed by the fact that housekeeping had not made the bed nor had they taken away the breakfast things and the room had a slightly sour smell to it tinged with body lotion and deodorant, until my acquaintance flung open the French windows and a blast of cold air swirled about, putting an end to any further intimacy that may or may not have occurred. Yes, shutting down and not opening up was the decision I had taken in Barcelona and I had returned to Australia whose name bore all the mysticism of the southern latitudes and lights and seascapes of unlimited beauty but which turned out to be just as small-minded as when I had left it many years ago, only now prejudice had been given licence by a lunatic in the White House and life had become too volatile on the streets and shutting down became a natural thing to do. This would not have been the case had Miranda been alive. For over thirty years

Miranda shared my ups and downs in my literary world, the guy, they said, they being the young, that had won more prizes than admirers. Then Miranda began shutting down and shutting herself away, as if she may have also believed the young, who were aspiring in their Oedipal way to kill the old guy and to steal his mantle, now glowing feebly or revealing the threadbare light of his pale skin through holey wool. But I have always been wrong in diagnosing isolation. Miranda had a cancer implanted by her parents and this obsessed her to the point of no return. The end was quicker than expected, after which I moved to Barcelona for a few years, traversing Europe in order to maintain a visa for teaching writers and actors, frauds and fakes, old Francoists, Catalans and masked Basques. Miranda had left a hole in me and I would never be whole again, having become an invisible professor, an absence discernible by a small breeze, a slight draft, my passing a vague memory of other times, conversations and a chattering of small fame. I've not looked at myself for some time. I'm anxious and fearful of something which I don't know about yet. It's hard to eke out what you don't know but can intimate to yourself that it's impending, just around the corner. Such time stamped by memory; such memory without time. Surely one day soon I'll die and everything will come to light. All these faces lit by Rembrandt's fireside in the soot of time. Nobody will know; or care who they were. Some corner we all inhabited for a small moment at the back of the stone wall. Meanwhile, the tincture of suspicion and plague linger over the old walking dead like me. I cannot look after everything anymore as in the past, those who used up my brief happiness that only lasted a nano-second. Those who had no thought but for themselves and I, who believed literature could be lived and shared, came up against the hard stone wall that it was only solitude which accounted for literature. That other him. Objectively passive. His whole library burned and in his auto-da-fé he had already renounced references, citations, page numbers, publication editions, and paraphrases. He was on his own. Burning out his former lives, wives, networks, preciosity, grooming of career, who now examines with meticulousness the lives of small animals, their relative brevity, their fates and death wishes when cornered. At one point he will give up on survival and its self.

I do not know, he says to himself. He thinks. He thinks too much. Never sleeping. Now that Eros is held in liam in the other room, he fades into ancient tapestries. He was real once – he will use a prolepsis – when he entered this guesthouse decades ago on a dirty weekend with spa and candles, now this fire-refuge, the music of heat and embers. He does not have that as a crutch now and understands the profound change that depleted one's being but brought about a softer body, one without muscle and with delicate skin. He who has lived two lives, a Jekyll and Hyde, one strained through sensitivity, the other through alcohol. He would have preferred the latter, rough, rambunctious. But now, this writing inside the head means a curtailing of the two remaining personalities. The fingerstyle of life leads to the skeletal clutch. Hell was other people, as Sartre took it from Dante and Dante from exile, and exile, as we all know, or those who were endowed with it, was taken from God's clay and deception. The mirror of a lie will always be a lie.

And then the young couple arrived. Both, it seemed, newly from Europe with a sophistication and boredom the great house had not embodied for a time, not since, at least, that other group from Paris, a high-level diplomatic delegation for a submarine commission, when it witnessed that Parisians did not travel well. He looked like a banker, soft, overfed, and cynically smart. He wore thick lenses and his introspection was finally assessed by our company that he was slightly deaf. She was underfed and pretty and when she introduced herself the old sat up as much as they could because elegance stirred like a familiar perfume the memories and fantasies which were never quite achieved in their own time. But these ephemera stirred nothing much else except curiosity and there was a greater drama outside as blue and white lights flashed and fire trucks raced up the dirt road. What of sex now? The dance of death?

The truth is that there was nothing connecting this new arrival to the rest of us who were now bonded together within this opulent chamber. (I thought of the violin sonata by Gabriel Pierné. Perhaps Proust's 'little phrase' may still perform its magic? I twiddled my thumbs; exercised my digits.) But no, they did not bring Paris with them. They were travelling and had been momentarily paused in their schedule by a natural disaster. We, however, were only focused on our disaster which we possessed as a group and would relinquish as soon as we returned to life. Would there have been a digression in which the camera eye moved into the bedroom of the Europeans, or concealed itself in a door-crack and recorded the boredom, the undressing and the tired but nervous conversation in the light of the fire? Could, as John Aubrey would have noticed, her husband have been made deaf and blind by too much of Venus? Curiosity about the lives of others, even if erotic, usually ends in boredom.

If your fifties are the crap decade, your sixties are not losses but minor decrepitudes, cellular exactitudes taken out on the body, along with incremental propitiations to you-know-what.

But the seventies – if you survived thus far without too many suicidal mishaps – is the age of insouciance. Laughter in the face of stress and frenzy. Too old for lusting after the young; not young enough for the backward arrow of time to elicit innocence, the seventies take comfort in letting things go, in not caring for phones and watches, currying a new excitement in seeing other people's tension at eye level, separated from the self and spotted statically floating in oceans of plastic distraction. The seventies is the decade of the cool castaway, though one could be rather blind both ocularly and alcoholically. Put both down to insouciance.

Here at the grand house in the middle of a bushfire we had cucumber sandwiches and unlabelled vintage wine for an early morning feast. I thought of Boccaccio during a plague, creating stories to cure melancholy, as I watched the French girl opposite me stretching out her silken legs on the chaise longue, and if her beauty was a 'yes', the message I was delivering was far more difficult: my epistolary cast of mind, composed of dead letters of desire, often scattered a confetti of celebratory microscripts without requite, that is, for the favour of my eyes in praise of beauty.

CRISTINA RIVERA GARZA
DEATH TAKES ME

...victims of the questions: who is killing me?
To whom am I giving myself over to be killed?

Translated by Sarah Booker and Robin Myers

Cristina Rivera Garza is the author of numerous works of poetry, fiction, and criticism. Recent and forthcoming publications in English translation include *Grieving: Dispatches from a Wounded Country,* a finalist for the National Book Critics Circle Award, *The Taiga Syndrome,* winner of the Shirley Jackson Award, and *New and Selected Stories*, out in April. Rivera Garza is Distinguished Professor and founder of the PhD Program in Creative Writing in Spanish at the University of Houston, Department of Hispanic Studies. In 2020, she was named a MacArthur Fellow in Fiction.

Sarah Booker is a literary translator and doctoral candidate in Hispanic Literature at the University of North Carolina Chapel Hill. Her translations include Cristina Rivera Garza's *The Iliac Crest* and *Grieving: Dispatches from a Wounded Country,* and Mónica Ojeda's *Jawbone*.

Robin Myers is a Mexico City-based translator and poet. Recent translations include *Copy* by Dolores Dorantes, *Another Life* by Daniel Lipara, *The Science of Departures* by Adalber Salas Hernández, and *The Restless Dead* by Cristina Rivera Garza.

The castrated men

> However, with humans, castration should not be understood as the basis for denying the possibility of the sexual relation, but as the prerequisite for any sexual relation at all. It can even be said that it is only because subjects are castrated that human relations as such can exist. Castration enables the subject to take others as Other rather than the same, since it is only after undergoing symbolic castration that the subject becomes preoccupied with questions such as 'what does the Other want?' and 'what am I for the Other?'
>
> *Renata Salecl*

What I believed I said

'That's a body,' I muttered to no one or to someone inside me or to nothing. I didn't recognise the words at first. I said something. And what I said or believed I said was for no one or for nothing or it was for me, who listened to myself from afar, from that deep inner place the air or light never reaches; where, hostile and greedy, the murmur began, the rushed, voiceless breath. A passageway. A forest. I said it after the alarm, after the incredulity. I said it when my eye was able to rest. After the long spell it took for me to give it form (something visible) (something utterable). I didn't say it: it came out of my mouth. The low voice. The tone of terror. Or of intimacy.

'Yes, it's a body,' I had to say, and instantly closed my eyes. Then, almost immediately, I opened them again. I had to say it. I don't know why. What for. But I looked up and, since I was exposed, I fell. Seldom the knees. My knees yielded to the weight of my body, and the vapour of my faltering breath clouded my vision. Trembling. There are trembling leaves and bodies.

Seldom the thundering of bones. Crick. On the pavement, to one side of the pool of blood, there. Crack. The folded legs, the insteps face-up, the palms of his hands. The pavement is made of miniscule rocks.

'It's a body,' I said or had to say, barely stammered, to no one or to me, who could not believe it, who refused to believe me, who never believed. Eyes open, disproportionately. The wail. Seldom the wail. That invocation. That crude prayer. I was studying it. There was no way out or cure for it. There was nothing inside and around me there was just a body. What I believed I said. A collection of impossible angles. A skin, the skin. Something on the asphalt. Knee. Shoulder. Nose. Something broken. Something dislocated. Ear. Foot. Sex. An open, red thing. A context. A boiling point. Something undone.

'A body,' I believed I said or barely muttered for no one or for me who was becoming a forest or passageway, an entrance orifice. Blackness. I believed I said. Seldom the lips that refuse to close. The shame. His final minute. His final image. His final complete sentence. The nostalgia for it all. Seldom. Staying still.

When I said again what I believed I said, when I said it to myself, who was the only person listening to me from that far-off inner place where the air and the light is generated and consumed, it was already too late: I had made the necessary calls, and because I had found him, I had already become the Informant.

My first body

No, I didn't know him.

No, I've never seen anything like it.

No.

It's difficult to explain what you do. It's difficult to tell someone as they interrogate you with a brown, vehement, crepuscular gaze that it's better, more interesting at least, to run through alleys than on the city streets. Is a city a cemetery? That it's even better to run there than on a track. A blue place. Something that isn't a lake. The knees are the problem, clearly. And the danger. It's difficult to confess to an official from the Department of Homicide Investigation that danger is, precisely, the allure. Or the unexpected. Something different. To detail, in all its slow dispersion, your daily routine, so that someone interested in something else, someone interested in solving a crime, will understand that running through the alleys of the city is a better alternative to running on tracks or illuminated sidewalks: that is a difficult thing. To tell her: that's really it, officer, the danger: what's hiding there: what doesn't happen elsewhere. It's difficult to speak in monosyllables.

I was running. I usually run at dusk. Also at dawn, but usually at dusk. I run on the track. I run from the coffee shop to my apartment. I avoid sidewalks and roads; I prefer shortcuts. Alleys. Narrow streets. No, I don't run for exercise. I run for pleasure. To get somewhere. I run, if you will, utilitarianly.

There's no time to say it. It wouldn't interest her. But running, this is what I think, is a mental thing. In every runner there should be a mind that runs. The goal is pleasure. The mind's challenge consists of staying in place: in the breathing, in the panting, in the knee, in the hand, in the sweat. If it goes elsewhere, it loses. If it wanders off, it loses even more. The mind's challenge is to be the body. If it aspires to it, if it achieves it, the mind then becomes the accomplice, and there, from that complicity, the detour that moves the mind and body away from boredom emerges. The detour is the pleasure. The goal.

Yes, sometimes there are dead cats. Pigeons. No, never men. Never women. No, none of that. This is my first body.

It's difficult to speak to you informally. Why would that be?

To see you: clean-shaven, white shirt, patent leather shoes. We know that everything is a cemetery. An apparition is always an apparition. You tell me nothing changes. Why shouldn't that be questioned? I'm sure you know how to whistle. You have that kind of mouth over the half-open mouth that neither air nor night comes through. My first.

Sometimes drug addicts. They share needles. They offer them. Yes.

No. I just run. That's all.

The endorphins, they explain to me, cause addiction. You start to run and then you can't stop. If that counts, then yes. Addict.

First there's the sensation of reality that prompts the falling onto your own two feet. Once. Again. Once and again. Measured, the trot. The steps. It's possible that someone runs away, frenzied. That intermittent relationship between the ground and the body – the weight of the two. Gravity and anti-gravity. A dialogue. A burning discussion. And the relationship, also intermittent, between the landscape and the mind. The silhouettes of the trees and the flow of the blood. Everything happens so quickly at the end, that's what they say. The colours of the cars and the more recent concern. The angles of the windows and the memory or the pain. All one life: the words: all one life. The struggle, always ferocious, to concentrate. I am here. I am now. That's called I Am My Breath. The internal sound. The rhythm. The weight. The scandalous murmur of the *I* within the dark fishbowl of the skeleton. But it's still so difficult to speak to you informally. Only later the loud noise. The ardour. The air that seems to thin out in the nasal cavities: narrow ridges in the lungs. An implosion. That violent way the endorphins are unleashed, producing a euphoria that in many ways resembles desire or love or pleasure. What will come of all this, my First? The lightness. The speed. The possibility of levitating. When I start running, that's the moment I'm searching for. That's the moment I pursue. That's the goal.

Yes, I write. Also. Also for pleasure, like running. To get somewhere. Utilitarianly. To get to the end of the page, I mean. Not for exercise. If you know what I mean: it's life or death.

It's difficult to explain what you do. The reasons. The consequences. The process. It's difficult to explain what you do without bursting into laughter or tears, uncontrollably. My eye is looking at me now, unguarded. Before the image of the murdered body that inserts itself like white noise into the interrogation; before what we no longer see but can't stop seeing, what the hell does it matter if we get to the end of the page or not? It's a rectangle, don't you see? I ask her. I'm not in any shape to say that doing this, getting to the end of the page, is a matter of life, matter of death. Where's the blood that proves it? you ask me. Where's my blood? you nod, perplexed.

No, I'd never seen him in the neighbourhood.

Yes, I do generally pay attention to those things. New faces. Lost pets. Businesses. Yes, personal, social interactions. But I hadn't seen him around here. No.

I'm sure.

Yes, I'm aware that he was missing a penis. Mutilation. Theft. Something that is not. I'm aware of all that.

Yes, it's a terrible thing against the dead.

I can't anymore.

I'm sure.

A terrible thing. Yes. Against the dead.

The poetry field of action

The Detective from the Department of Homicide Investigation showed me a photograph of the bricks in the wall outside the Chinese restaurant, specifically the bricks from the corner where the restaurant ends and behind which the Alley of the Castrated Man unfolds with its monumental narrowness. They were already calling it that. It was almost immediate. The bricks, I couldn't help but notice, were covered with the unreal light that often gets me out of the house and demands I inhale the air of the world at 6:15 in the evening. All this in the city.

'Do you recognise this?' the official asked with her gaze on the bridge of my nose, the tips of my eyelashes. Without taking my eyes off the box, I fell silent. I looked. I examined.

They weren't hard to find. These diminutive words, painted

with coral-coloured nail polish, were there, on that corner, under that hypothetical light, over the uneven texture of a brick:

> beware of me, my love
> beware of the silent woman in the desert
> of the traveller with an emptied glass
> and of her shadow's shadow

'Quite literary, don't you think?' the Detective insisted into my silence. 'Your field of action, am I right?'

I smiled at her because I had never thought of poetry as a 'field of action', and because Alejandra Pizarnik's lines were indeed present in a sudden here and now, a great, terrible thing against the dead. A deed. Rage in diminutive letters. Something tiny.

I didn't look at her. I avoided looking at her. I kept staring at the photograph. I saw something else instead, you always see something else. I saw the images of an installation: *Great Deeds Against the Dead*, 1994. Fibreglass, resin, paint, artificial hair, 277 x 244 x 152 centimetres. Jake and Dinos Chapman, born in the sixties, had arranged three life-sized male figures around a trunk. Tied and naked, arranged in positions with vaguely religious resonances (a crucified body, open arms), the men hanging from the trunks were missing their genitals. I saw that. There, where a penis and testicles should have been, in their place, was tarnished, earthly flesh. Absence in red. Castration. All of it enveloped in the acrid stench of blood. All that in London. Jake and Dinos Chapman had declared to the press that they conceptualised themselves as a pair of sore-eyed scopophiliac oxymorons. Jake and Dinos Chapman claimed they were artists. I saw something else, and because of that, I saw you. A city is always a cemetery.

We were in the Detective's office – a basement trembling with the sound of uneven voices and the blank velocity of papers passed from hand to hand – and, perhaps because of that, the miniscule words in nail polish seemed both more threatening and funnier. A children's story. That type of cruelty. In this place where it felt like no light but the artificial kind could reach, where the Detective's eyes surely got used to their own opacity, the words of Alejandra Pizarnik made it so that the world out there, the world that had killed her, seemed benign or banal.

'They're brutal words,' I finally told her, looking her in the eye, accepting her challenge. '*The traveller with an emptied glass*,' I repeated as if I were reciting it before a hushed crowd made up entirely of children, '*of her shadow's shadow,*' I enunciated, slowly, as I realised that the Detective's dark brown eyes, insistently watching me, full of concentration, the type of concentration that has always made me think of a mind while writing, were lit up just then. 'Pizarnik always did that really well. Said brutal things.'

The Detective smiled at me. An echo. Something distant.

'I knew it,' she said, a strange inflection in some part of her voice as her hand leapt to my right elbow, lightly guiding my body, gracefully even, towards the way out of her basement. 'I knew you and I would talk a lot about poetry.'

It wasn't until after, long after, that I understood: the last thing she said was not an invitation but a threat.

When I reached the door to my apartment, as I turned the

key for the third time to the left, I wondered if she'd been there, too. The installation hadn't been in the city all that long ago, and I'm sure this is why the phrase I'd uttered in the Detective's basement, probably at random, evoked the memory: *Great Deeds Against the Dead*. An incomplete, biased, real translation. An echo of Goya. A reverberation of the war. Great things, yes, terrible things against the dead. That touch us. Deeds against them. *Beware of me, my love*. I wondered if the Detective had also seen it or if she had only been referencing the engraving. The original. Francisco de Goya y Lucientes: *Sad forebodings of what is going to happen. Bury them and keep quiet. There is no time left. Even worse. This is too much. This is worse. Great Deed! With dead men! I saw it. This is bad. The worst is too big. What is the use of a cup? The results. Truth has died. This is how it happened.*

I wondered if maybe she hadn't seen anything. If it had been nothing but a great coincidence.

As the door slowly gave way to the key's clumsy buffeting, I remembered that Goya had said all that on a metal sheet. The titles like scraps of dialogue among the dead. The pencil wet with special ink on a plate protected with powdered resin. Then the heat, and the resin just adhered to the metal, producing a granular surface. All this in a city named Madrid. The wake of the resistance against the invasion of a man named Bonaparte. An uprising: eighty-five metal sheets, forty-five on the massacre and sixteen on the famine that, a couple years later, caused twenty thousand deaths, his wife's among them. *Fatal consequences of the war*. That's what Goya said. The metal plate coated with varnish and then, within the acid, only within the acid, the grooves marked in copper. The lesion emerged. The fingers of my imagination touched it, that lesion, in the static air of the apartment, when I was finally inside. The illuminated lesion. My eyes fell on it once and again. The cut. The fissure. Obsessive, my eyes. Incapable of seeing anything else. Blind to anything else. I fell onto the couch. Seldom the knees. My bag on the ground. The air that finally escaped through my mouth. I don't know how to whistle. I remembered that. Then I wondered, there, immobile, curled up on the soft surface of the sofa (my left cheek on the seat) (my right hand hanging, orphaned, almost touching the floor), if the Detective, who surely had been there, at the much talked about exposition of the Chapman brothers, would have held, with a delicacy I found difficult to picture, the tall glass of champagne as she strolled around, with the tired tone of someone who has already seen it all, with that smug or prudent indifference, how incredible, how shockingly incredible it always was to see, regardless whether it was Goya or the Chapman brothers, an etching or an installation or a real event, the body of a castrated man. I wondered, still curled up there, my knees almost at my mouth, my right hand now brushing the floor, if the Detective, who had just barely finished interrogating me with great meticulousness and without any sign of tiring, with a discipline so fierce that it seemed not particularly human, had enjoyed the cocktail. The bubbles of the champagne. The light vaporous seething inebriation. The murmurs.

Victim is always feminine

It was after the third murder that the Detective sought me out again. She called me, and we arranged to meet in the café next to the Chinese restaurant. When I arrived, still panting after my fifteen-minute sprint, she was already waiting for me with an Americano – no sugar – on the empty side of the table. Her fingers drumming the beat of an old melody. The instantaneous impression that the woman lived inside a house with green walls, followed immediately by the impression that the woman didn't have a house. No walls around her.

'So you're still running,' she commented with that strange accent in some corner of her voice, on its outskirts, almost. In response, I nodded and moved towards the bar to say hello to the owner and ask for a glass of water.

Someone runs, I told you, convinced that everything was a cemetery. Later I acted as if nothing were happening. As if you weren't happening.

'Am I interrupting your work?' she asked as she swivelled her seat around. It was clear she was no expert in the field of insipid small talk and was impatient to get to the point and address the matter that had brought us there, face to face in a frank attitude of expectation.

'My work is a continuous interruption,' I answered drolly, irresponsibly, trying to avoid the topic because I found myself – but the Detective had no way of knowing this – in one of those silent, unproductive cycles that, on other occasions, mostly before I picked up running, had sent me out to directly observe, in an obsessive immobility, the sky.

'I suppose you're already aware,' she whispered and bent over her cup of coffee just to have the opportunity to look up from there. An abyss in her movement.

'It's been in all the papers,' I confirmed.

'An interesting case, don't you think?'

I thought – and here to think really means to produce an image – about the castrated bodies of the three young men who had appeared, naked and bloody, on the city's asphalt. I thought – and here to think really means to hear the echo – about the word castration and all the tragic references of the term. I thought – and here to think really means to see – about how long, about how interminable, about how incessant the word dis-mem-ber-ment was. I thought – and here to think means to quietly pronounce – about the term serial murders and I realised it was the first time I connected it with the male body. And I thought – and here to think really means to practice irony – that it was interesting in and of itself how, at least in Spanish, the word victim, or víctima, is always feminine.

'Are you laughing?' the Detective interrupted. Intrigued. Annoyed.

And it was right then that I thought, in the most untimely way, just like those clear days that appear amid the ashen ones preceding the explosion of springtime, that the asesino, the murderer, was really an asesina, a murderess.

And then I saw you out of the corner of my eye, like someone waiting to reach a difficult agreement. Like someone hopelessly waiting in a train station; like someone. The train passing by. The hand, shaken.

'It's the word víctima, Detective,' I explained without any hope of being understood as I wrote the definite article and the noun on a paper napkin. '*La* víctima is always feminine. Do you see? In the recounting of the facts, in the newspaper articles, in the essays that will be written about these events, this word will castrate them over and over again.'

Over and over again. The echo. Over. Over again. The repetition. The sonorous phenomenon occurred, we both realised, when the café owner softly sang *Gee baby, ain't I good to you*, and the coincidence, the dark humour of the coincidence, provoked a burst of laughter that I couldn't repress.

'And that's funny to you?'

'The song on the radio?' I asked, trying unsuccessfully to draw her attention to what had just happened on the threshold of her ears. It can take so much work to listen to a song. I thought that. I thought: it takes so much effort to believe what's before your eyes. And then, out of pure pleasure, I winked at you.

'The castration. The double castration,' the Detective clarified, concentrating on her objective and deaf to everything else.

'No,' I told her after giving it some thought. 'No, I don't find it funny at all.'

I'm sure I was telling the truth.

Then, without any transition, as if the Detective were rigorously following a screenplay I hadn't read but was participating in, she said: 'This was found in the hand of the second body,' and placed on the table a white sheet of paper within which or on which someone had arranged a series of letters clipped from newspapers or magazines, making them, then, in the act itself, castrated letters, and simultaneously establishing not the absence but what was absent within the sheet. It was, of course, another Alejandra Pizarnik poem:

NOW THEN: Who will stop plunging their hands in search of tributes for the forgotten girl? The cold will pay. The wind will pay. As will the rain. And the thunder. *For Aurora and Julio Cortázar.*

I looked at it again, slowly, unable to believe that a woman so professional in appearance had just placed a sheet of paper that was a piece of evidence in my hands. The original. I ran my fingertips over its surface. I brought it close to my nose, expecting a peculiar aroma. The tribute. The plunging hands.

'*Diana's Tree*,' I murmured without thinking about it, without really knowing how it was that I knew it or why I remembered it so clearly. '1962.'

'You know it?' the Detective immediately asked, and I couldn't help but note she hadn't called it a 'poem' or a 'line'.

'Everyone knows it,' I told her, oblivious to the arrogance. 'Everyone in the poetry field of action,' I corrected myself. And before looking at the photograph in which the third Pizarnikian message appeared, I also couldn't help but see that on the very surface of the name Cortázar there were hiding, threatening, a *cortar* and an *azar*, a *cut* and a *fate* – words that, in that moment, lacked all innocence.

The third message, written in lipstick on the sidewalk, said:

she says she doesn't know the fear of death of love
she says she fears the death of love
she says love is death is fear
she says death is fear is love
she says she doesn't know

The photograph of a poem. That's what I had in my hands: the photograph of a poem. To realise that I had the photograph of a poem in my hands sparked a strange rage in me. Something like a shadow passed over the roof. That's what some call melancholia. Or tree. Isn't that true? Alejandra Pizarnik's words left you mute for a long time, that's what I perceived.

'Tell me, please, Cristina, who is the "everyone" who knows this kind of poetry so well?' And then I looked at the Detective again as if I'd just come back from a long journey or woken up from a very dark dream. Poetry. *This kind of poetry*.

I and who I was

I've said it several times, both in public and in private: I do not lead an interesting life. Though many would say that my field of action, as the Detective called it, is fiction, I've always secretly believed that my field, my action, belongs to poetry. Although this is because I consider poetry, in the most traditional and hierarchical sense, to be the crown of all writing, the goal of all writing, I rarely admit it to myself, much less in front of others. To accept such a thing would provoke great shame and great sorrow in me. To avoid both sensations, I tend to say that I'm a professor and that I like to run. If the questions continue, I may go on to admit that I write, and frequently, but I omit the titles and the number of books I've published. If pressed, I acknowledge that I like the peace of my office and the warmth of my apartment, especially the big bedroom windows that overlook the park where, with similar conviction, if total chaos, the poplars and pine trees grow. In any case, whether or not I say so in ceding to questions from others, it would be quite reasonable to describe my life as stable. Other equally precise adjectives would be: comfortable, relaxed, routine, pleasant. It surprised me that the Lover with the Luminous Smile would believe, even for a fleeting instant, that I could be a suspect of such cruel crimes, it's true, but I didn't mind. His light joke indicated to me that in some part of his head or desire he conceived of me or produced me as a woman that, being me, was really another person. A serial killer. Someone with sufficient cruelty or frustration or madness to attack men and violently, furiously, or indifferently cut off their genitals.

Someone with sufficient physical force to drag the dismembered bodies down narrow alleys or along dark sidewalks. Someone, too, with sufficient delicacy to transcribe, with fingernail polish or lipstick, entire poems by Alejandra Pizarnik. Someone with abysses under their wrists. Someone with complicated eyes and tremulous hands. The hatred. The revenge. That the Lover with the Luminous Smile could consider me, again, even for the most fleeting of instants, even within the conspiratorial humour that precedes amorous sessions, a castrator, is something I found quite hilarious. So hilarious that I let out a long cackle and kissed him full on the mouth. So hilarious that I bit his nipples and pulled his thick mat of hair with a tenderness I only began to feel just then. It's truly strange, I told you, how tenderness crops up sometimes. But as you weren't there, you didn't hear. As if to guide his hand towards my pubis as I mounted his hips. To pronounce the words: 'These are two bodies.' Enough to sustain, a little while later, a meditative silence at the very moment when he closed his eyes and exhaled, with delight, with a grimace of pain, with something like delirium, the breath of his pleasure. That. The last one.

I can still see myself looking at him: a body within another, interwoven, exhausted. His sex engulfed by mine. Great deeds, yes. Two bodies.

I can still hear the howl of the wind. And I blink. Once. And again. The goosebumps from what I observe: the absence. The unprecedented castration. From what cannot be observed. I still await the coming of blood. A drop. A flow. The dizziness. The weeping of the next of kin. The news of the death. The general stupefaction. I am still infuriated by the curious onlookers who lean out to see, to see you on the inside. To save themselves.

I'm still moved by the words that descended in droves, uninvited, and settled on the pillow:

now
        at this innocent hour
the one I used to be sits with me
along my peripheral vision

How to read poetry

When she asked, I told her the truth: I wasn't an expert on the subject. I had indeed read Alejandra Pizarnik – first because of the morbid curiosity inspired by the image of a suicidal poet; then because her books were difficult to find, making them expensive cult objects; later, almost at the end, out of pleasure. That's what I said: out of pleasure. And then I added: out of terror. Because she uttered words that got lodged in my throat. Because she made her vertiginous descent into musical, bloody infernos that made me feel, frankly, as much attraction as fear. Because she played.

The Detective looked at me suspiciously. She rose from the chair in front of my desk and began, without asking permission, to examine all the books on the shelves that almost entirely covered the walls of the office. Her hand like a brush on the spines.

'Do you remember the second man's poem?' she asked. Before I had time to answer, she added, her back still to me: 'The cold will pay. The wind will pay. As will the rain. And the thunder.'

Her reasoning turned out to be obvious: there was a warning

in these words, a sign she wanted to follow. A clue. I didn't laugh this time, but I did stand up.

'You don't read poetry like that,' I whispered, increasingly dumbfounded. 'Poetry isn't denotative. It isn't like a manual,' I was going to continue, but she interrupted me with a firm voice, and if I hadn't known she was an officer in service of the Department of Homicide Investigation, I still would have recognised it as the voice of an expert.

'But according to what I've read,' she said, turning her face towards me in a dramatic circular movement, 'it can be prophetic. At least that's what some poets believe. That it has the power of prophecy.'

Defeated, I returned to my side of the desk and fell into the chair. If you'd been there, resting each of your palms on each of my shoulders, I would have been able to laugh. I would have been able to tell her: what I want is to stop seeing it. The noise of the wind seeped, as it had been doing for days, through the bottom crack of the window, and the sound automatically made me uneasy, an unnecessary internal turbulence. I wondered, though I wasn't prepared to think about this kind of thing, if another man might die right then. If that man might be bathed in blood right now. Before me. The Detective, meanwhile, pulled out the complete collection of poetry by Alejandra Pizarnik, edited by Ana Becciú and published by Editorial Lumen, and she proceeded to read the back cover aloud, as if she were alone in my office, or as if she were the owner of the book:

Born in Buenos Aires in 1936, Alejandra Pizarnik published her first poems when she was just twenty years old. In the early 1960s, she spent several years living in Paris, where she developed friendships with André Pierre de Mandiargues, Octavio Paz, Julio Cortázar, and Rosa Chacel. Upon her return to Buenos Aires, she dedicated the rest of her life to writing. She died in Buenos Aires on September 25, 1972.

Without pausing, she continued with fragments from the back cover:

One of the most emblematic figures of Hispanic literature, controversial, polemical, who became a myth among adolescents in the eighties and nineties...deep intimacy and severe sensuality...intense insomnia and midday lucidity...her poems spread love and fear everywhere.

'The rain,' she interrupted herself, not closing the book, as if she hadn't realised that a new idea had come into her head and that she was, in fact, interrupting herself. 'The cold. The thunder. Don't you think the next murder will happen in the rainy season?'

I hope I looked at her with the unease and incredulity I felt inside. Surely it was those two moods or those two emotions that led me directly to the irony.

'Officer, do you even know when the rainy season in Buenos Aires is? I mean,' I added, 'after all, Alejandra was talking about the Southern Cone.'

The Detective closed the book, took her jacket from the coat rack, and winked her left eye.

'Don't be so literal,' she said, just before opening the door, winking her left eye. 'You don't read poetry like that. But thanks for the tip.'

And that's how, without even asking for permission, the Detective began to speak with me informally.

The cutting adjective

The eyes: big, inhabited, dark, close together, curious.
The hands: long, fine, bony, soft, amber-coloured, pianistic.
The hair: salt-and-pepper, gleaming, short.
The mouth: flesh of my flesh, grooved, open, nervous.
The voice: from another world, level with the floor, sudden.
The sigh: emphatic, obvious, sexual.
The skin: weightless.
The beard: thick, trimmed, masculine.
The gaze: netlike, embracing, what do you want from me?
The question: is it you?

The sky: open, dry, jagged, blue.

The answer: sometimes.
The laughter: funny, cautious, deep, divine. A bird over a marble tower.

The hand: on the shoulder, at the waist, caressing.

The wink: unexpected, angular, inclined.
The breath: lavender, heno de pravia, April wind. Mint. Childhood.
The laughter: interminable, discrete, it-approaches.
The gaze from afar: a bridge on the verge of collapse, a vine nearly snapped, a cry for help, a woman tied to train tracks, an oracle, an investigation, a telescope.
The gaze from up close: a stabbing pain, a match, a burn, an ardour.
The stride: zigzagging, defaulting, dubious.

The question: is it my voice?
The answer: it is mine.

The noise: protective.
The alcohol: cold, banal, an anchor, a door, a button.
The voice: still from another world, distinct, multifaceted, deceitful, deep, guttural.
The hands: long, soft, bony, amber-coloured, pianistic, on the iliac crests.

The order: follow me.

The fingernails: trimmed, clean, closed letters.
The mouth: full, open, eager, nervous, imperial, drooling, wider open, denotative, with nothing-beyond.
The hands: on the hands, against the wall, keys. Locks.
The breath: electronica music.
The gaze: boiling, netlike, skylike, nightlike.
The hands: in the sex on the sex under the sex behind the sex.
The chin: on the left shoulder.
The mouth: ah, the mouth. The ear. The neck. The hair.
The sex: the sex.

The question: is it your body?
The answer: and mine.

The intellectual interruption: only the hounding of death hurls us so furiously towards the unfamiliar body.

The poem castrated by its own language

The Detective called very early because she wanted to discuss the subject of castration in some poems by Alejandra Pizarnik. She said it just like that, without preamble or explanation; she said it literally, with an overtly neutral tone: I want to talk to you about castration in some poems by Alejandra Pizarnik.

'Over lunch?' I asked sarcastically, trying to underscore the poor taste entailed by bringing food to your mouth while talking, with that same mouth, about penises and testicles severed from their bodies. I couldn't understand why she sought me out so zealously; what good would my answers do.

'Yes,' she answered, overlooking the malice in my remark. 'The usual place?'

When I arrived, as with our previous meetings, she was already there, waiting for me. Her eyes fixed on the door, her fingers drumming nervously on the table. She could hardly wait for me to sit down before handing me the menu.

'Let's order,' she said, treating the food as what it was, a mere pretext to our true main course – castration.

'So you still don't have any suspects?' I couldn't place why I was so eager to irritate her, but when she snapped the menu closed, I knew I'd succeeded. The Detective was not in a good mood.

'It's a difficult case,' she explained, admirably maintaining her composure as she raised her hands and let them move, for the first time since I'd been meeting with her, with some sort of grace, some sort of emphasis in the air. 'Full of psychological nooks and crannies. Of poetic shadows. Gender traps. Metaphors. Metonyms,' and as she uttered the last word, she bowed her head, then looked up from that position. Her body facing down. Her gaze looking up. That clash of directions. I'd seen her do this several times before, but it wasn't until that moment that I understood it was her warning sign. Then the ironic smile appeared on her face: the thin corner that rose, in sync with her suddenly expressive hands, towards her temples.

'Transnominations,' I murmured, settling into those words that weren't hers but mine. Feeling like an imposture of myself, I ordered a bottle of water from a busy waiter.

The Detective pulled some copies from her black briefcase. These partially wrinkled pages were printed with 'On this night in this world,' the Pizarnik poem that was published, as she informed me just then, in the *Gaceta del Fondo de Cultura* in July 1972. The Detective placed the pages on the table. Pointing at the underlined passage, she asked: 'So every poem fails?'

She was asking as if I were wondering the same thing. She asked with the kind of knowledge forged in strange and uncomfortable coincidences around a glass of water or a belt where countless suitcases circulate as if part of the same eternity. She asked with my words. This is a Great Kingdom that is missing a queen or a king. And I, for a moment, for just a second, believed we were understanding each other.

on this night in this world
words of the dream of childhood of death
it's never what you wish to say
the mother-tongue castrates
the tongue is an organ of knowledge
about the failure of every poem
castrated by its own tongue

which is the organ of re-creation
of re-cognition
but not of resurrection.

I read carefully. I read with the kind of knot in my throat that threatens to become a domestic animal. I read and had to pour myself the first glass of water. How could I tell the Detective that every poem is the inability of language to produce the presence in itself that, by simply being language, is all absence? How could I communicate to the Detective that the poem's task is not to communicate but quite the opposite: to protect the secret place that resists all communication, all transmission, every effort of translation? How could I tell her, without choking on the sip of water and the sadness that rose in me upon realising, again and again, that the tongue will never be an organ of resurrection, that words, as Pizarnik says a few lines later, in a declaration no less gloomy for its accuracy, 'do not make love / they make absence'? How could I explain to this woman, so firm, so well uniformed, that while she pointed her short immaculate fingernail to the word *castrated* in a poem about the uselessness, the inutility of all poems, all I could do was reminisce about the language that is all memory and, in being memory, is all absence, the contour of the body and the sex of that thin beautiful boy with a thick, manly beard, that had appeared, literally out of nowhere, out of the nowhere that is sometimes the absence of the absence of language, declaring, in the most jocular and lighthearted way, that he was Sometimes-Him? How could I not read aloud, in the most tremulous voice, 'where does this conspiracy of invisibilities come from?' without causing that old shame she will never understand, the shame that isn't wounding her, as it wounds Pizarnik, in her 'first person singular'? How could I tell the Detective, stop here, at these lines: 'what did you do with the gift of sex? / oh, all my dead – / i ate them i choked / i've had enough of enough,' read carefully, see for yourself, again and again, confirm it, and use the same informal command, again and yet again, do you see how one goes on 'wasting the gifts of the body'?

But in the end I decided to ask you all that, because over time you learn to pose questions to someone who can actually answer them. Your silence, of course, filled me with pity.

'I just asked you, rhetorically, as you professor types say, if every poem is a failure,' the Detective remarked with a certain tremor in her voice that became unequivocally hers. 'It wasn't so you'd start crying, Cristina.'

When she refilled my glass with water and placed it in front of me, I had to accept that, sooner rather than later, sooner than ever, the Detective and I were going to talk about poetry.

One day, without a doubt, we would.

Clear light

At the beginning of March, on a day with clear light, the fourth man appeared.

Dismembered. No genitals. Covered in blood. A few young men who had gone camping on the outskirts of the city found him on the shore of a lake. When they got out of their truck, they noticed the smell and the buzz of flies behind the brush.

'There must be a dead guy over there,' they'd said, with that premonition that sometimes comes with dark humour, the class clown.

When they approached and saw it, two of them vomited.

It took two others thirty or forty-five more seconds to put the pieces together and form, from what was scattered on the ground, the body of a man. The puzzle of a body.

It was the youngest who called the police.

And then the terror and the clear light of early March became one.

They found the line from the poem later, during the first examinations. The Detective and the Detective's Assistant couldn't help but recognise the beauty in the phrase and the beauty in the composition of the phrase. And the macabre precision of the phrase: that beauty.

'It's true, death takes me in the throes of sex.'

Each word sketched this time with the (elongated) (smooth) (flat) stones of the adjacent lake. The art of the earth. Forms of procedural composition.

Messages under the door

Everything would have stayed on track, which is often a track towards oblivion, if it hadn't been for the apparition of the messages under the door. In the beginning of the period I called the period of the Castrated Men, there was nothing but a generalised apprehension that made me suspect everyone, especially lovers of contemporary art. Then, as the days passed, the indifference – impulsive, sagacious, cruel – emerged. As we know, it's impossible to live in a state of perpetual terror.

As we know, when terror is permanent, the body finds or produces protective mechanisms among which the impossibility of feeling, the impossibility of paying attention, the impossibility of articulating nonsense, are frequent. I had already found myself in this stage of denial when I picked up the first message that appeared on my apartment floor.

I remember everything: it was cold, a cold that was quite unusual in April and for which, therefore, I had not prepared myself either physically or psychologically. I returned from my office as I always did, on foot, hurriedly, almost jogging, savouring the anticipation of my warm room, my silent ceilings, the surrounding calm. I opened the door then, in a state of total helplessness. That's how I saw it. I realised it. I went towards it. It was a sheet of bright white paper folded in four almost-perfect sections. The writing, in a dark reddish ink, an ink that looked as if it were made from a thick wine, from an almost blood-and-bone wine, was steady, stable, pretty. On that paper and in that ink, on one of the four almost-perfect sections, was my full name: cristina rivera garza. All in lower case. Then, on the sheet, in handwriting that feigned calm, not haste, the message said:

'i want to talk to you. will i be able to?'

The message, of course, was unsigned. It came, in fact, without any identifying information other than the shape and colour of the handwriting, the choice of lower-case letters, and the brevity of its challenge. *Will I be able to?* I asked myself for a long time. Motionless. In a state contrary to anticipation. I asked myself silently and out loud. I asked myself and the window in which my reflection, distorted, asked me at the same time. I asked the landscape, confusing the evening poplars with tall European elms. Will I be able to? A long time passed in this very way.

Translations of Alejandra Pizarnik come from the following sources: *Diana's Tree*, translated by Yvette Siegert, and *Extracting the Stone of Madness: Poems 1962–1972*, translated by Yvette Siegert.

The Novel Prize 2022

The Novel Prize is a biennial award for a book-length work of literary fiction written in English by published and unpublished writers around the world. The prize recognises works which explore and expand the possibilities of the form, and are innovative and imaginative in style. It offers US$10,000 to the winner and simultaneous publication by Giramondo Publishing in Australia and New Zealand, by Fitzcarraldo Editions in the United Kingdom and Ireland, and by New Directions in North America. *Cold Enough for Snow* by Jessica Au, the inaugural winner, was unanimously chosen from over 1500 entries. It is out now in English and forthcoming in fifteen languages around the world.

Visit thenovelprize.com for more information.

Submissions open in April 2022.

Fitzcarraldo Editions

Jessica Au
Cold Enough for Snow

A young woman has arranged a holiday with her mother in Japan. They travel by train, visit galleries and churches, eat together in small cafés and restaurants and walk along the canals at night, aware of the autumn rain and the prospect of snow. They talk, or seem to talk: about the weather, horoscopes, memories; about the mother's family in Hong Kong, and the daughter's own formative experiences. How much is spoken between them, how much is thought but not spoken? *Cold Enough for Snow* is a reckoning and an elegy: with extraordinary skill, Au creates an enveloping atmosphere that expresses both the tenderness between mother and daughter, and the distance between them.

'An intricate and multi-layered work of art – a complex and profound meditation on identity, familial bonds and our inability to fully understand ourselves, those we love and the world around us.' *Books + Publishing*

'Flawed understanding, consolation, and insufficiency all infuse this compelling, unsettling novel reminiscent of Jhumpa Lahiri's *Whereabouts* or Rachel Cusk's Outline Trilogy. A beautifully observed book, written in precise, elegant prose that contains a wealth of deep feeling. A beautifully observed book, written in precise, elegant prose that contains a wealth of deep feeling.' *Kirkus*, starred review

Recent titles from Giramondo

Fiction
Jessica Au *Cold Enough for Snow*
Max Easton *The Magpie Wing*
Zarah Butcher-McGunnigle *Nostalgia Has Ruined My Life*
Pip Adam *Nothing to See*
Fiona Kelly McGregor *Buried Not Dead*

Non-fiction
Evelyn Juers *The Dancer: A Biography for Philippa Cullen*
Gerald Murnane *Last Letter to a Reader*
Vanessa Berry *Gentle and Fierce*
Anwen Crawford *No Document*
Nicholas Jose and Benjamin Madden *Antipodean China: Reflections on Literary Exchange*

Poetry
Adam Aitken *Revenants*
J. S. Harry *New and Selected Poems*
Andy Jackson *Human Looking*
Eunice Andrada *Take Care*
Jane Gibian *Beneath the Tree Line*
Toby Fitch *Sydney Spleen*
Song Lin *The Gleaner Song*
Mark Anthony Cayanan *Unanimal, Counterfeit, Scurrilous*
Kristen Lang *Earth Dwellers*

For more information visit giramondopublishing.com/books/

Acknowledgements

We respectfully acknowledge the Gadigal, Burramattagal and Cammeraygal peoples, the traditional owners of the lands where Giramondo's offices are located. We extend our respects to their ancestors and to all First Nations peoples and Elders.

HEAT Series 3 Number 1 has been prepared in collaboration with Ligare Book Printers, Avon Graphics, Ball & Doggett paper suppliers and Candida Stationery – we thank them for their support.

The Giramondo Publishing Company is grateful for the support of Western Sydney University in the implementation of its book publishing program.

Giramondo Publishing is assisted by the Australian Government through the Australia Council for the Arts.

HEAT Series 3
Editor Alexandra Christie
Designer Jenny Grigg
Typesetter Andrew Davies
Digital Producer Alice Desmond
Copy Editor Aleesha Paz
Social Media Coordinator Kate Prendergast
Publishers Ivor Indyk and Evelyn Juers
Associate Publisher Nick Tapper

Editorial Advisory Board

Contact

For editorial enquiries, please email heat.editor@giramondopublishing.com.
Follow us on Instagram @HEAT.lit and Twitter @HEAT_journal.

Accessibility

We understand that some formats will not be accessible to all readers. If you are a reader with specific access requirements, please contact orders@giramondopublishing.com.

For more information, visit giramondopublishing.com/heat.

First published 2022
from the Writing and Society Research Centre
at Western Sydney University
by the Giramondo Publishing Company
PO Box 752
Artarmon NSW 1570 Australia
www.giramondopublishing.com

Typeset in Tiempos and Founders Grotesk Condensed
designed by Kris Sowersby at Klim Type Foundry

Printed and bound by Ligare Book Printers
Distributed in Australia by NewSouth Books

A catalogue record for this book is available from
the National Library of Australia.

HEAT Series 3 Number 1
ISBN: 978-1-922725-00-4
ISSN: 1326-1460

ISBN 978-1-922725-00-4
9 781922 725004 >